MATTER OF FACT

CJFallon

Published by
C J FALLON
Lucan Road
Palmerstown
Dublin 20
Ireland

First printing August 2001
This Reprint June 2003

Acknowledgements

The publishers gratefully acknowledge the following for permission to reproduce copyright material:

Bord Fáilte - Irish Tourist Board; Courtesy of The National Gallery of Ireland and the Jesuit Community who acknowledge the generosity of the late Dr Marie Lea-Wilson; Courtesy of the estate of Roderic O'Conor; Courtesy of the estate of Mainie Jellett; The National Museum of Ireland; Gianni Dagli Orti/CORBIS; The Aillwee Caves; Archivo Iconografico S.A./CORBIS; Buddy Mays/CORBIS; Jay Syverson/CORBIS; D. Robert & Lorri Franz/CORBIS; Dr Milton Reisch/CORBIS; Bord na Mona Plc; Anne Behan, Kildare; Ken Maye, Kildare; Mary Evans Picture Library; Lake County Museum/CORBIS; Bettmann/CORBIS; Brian Vikander/CORBIS; GOAL; Bóthar; Neal Preston/CORBIS; Hulton-Deutsch Collection/CORBIS; Hellest Adrune/CORBIS;Trapper Frank/CORBIS; Shamin Ferdaus/CORBIS; Attar Maher/SYGMA; The Orion Publishing Group Ltd; Inpho Photography; Kit de Fever/SYGMA; The Random House Group Ltd; Michael S Yamashita/CORBIS; Papilio/CORBIS; Wolfgang Kaehler/CORBIS; Pictures courtesy of An Garda Siochana; Catherine Karnow/CORBIS; Irish Ferries.

Every effort has been made to secure permission to reproduce copyright material in this book. If the publishers have inadvertently overlooked any copyright holders, however, they will be pleased to come to a suitable arrangement with them at the earliest opportunity.

Contents

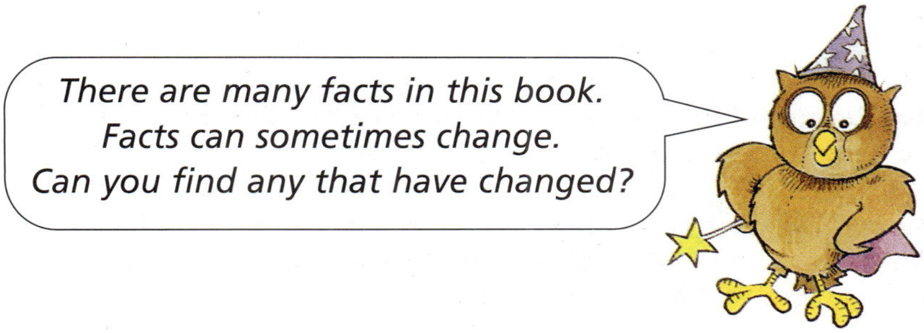

There are many facts in this book.
Facts can sometimes change.
Can you find any that have changed?

Aoife's tale

In the novel, *Strongbow*, by Morgan Llewelyn, Strongbow, is just a boy. He is terrified in his first battle against the 'savages' in Wales. However, Strongbow grew up to become a fierce Norman knight. It was not long before he would invade Ireland and change the country forever.

Aoife O'Brien and her twin brother, Richard, were on a class trip to the National Gallery of Ireland. Aoife expected to be very bored. She had only once been to an art gallery during a holiday in Paris. Her Dad had taken her to the Louvre Museum to see the *Mona Lisa*. The painting was much smaller than she had imagined. She could not understand what all the fuss was about!

The National Gallery of Ireland

Aoife knew that their teacher, Mr Harrison, would probably linger for ages, giving the history of every painting. 'If you are well behaved, we'll go for a burger afterwards,' promised Mr Harrison, as he shepherded the class into the first room. But Aoife was not listening.

'Wow!', she whispered, as she stared at the biggest picture she had ever seen. It took up an entire wall of the enormous room in which they were standing.

'This painting is known as *The Marriage of Strongbow and Aoife*,' Mr Harrison announced. 'It was painted in 1854 by one of Ireland's most famous painters, Daniel Maclise (1806-70). It **depicts** a famous scene from Irish history.'

'I was afraid of that,' moaned Richard.

'Strongbow was a **Norman knight**,' Mr Harrison continued. 'His real name was Richard de Clare. He was nicknamed "Strongbow" because of his great strength when using the **longbow**.'

'Aoife's Dad, Diarmaid Mac Murrough, was the king of Leinster. In 1166, his arch-enemy, Tiernan O'Rourke, defeated Diarmaid Mac Murrough in a battle. Diarmaid knew that he was in danger of losing his kingdom. He had no friends in Ireland to help him to fight the O'Rourkes. He turned instead to King Henry II of England and France for help.'

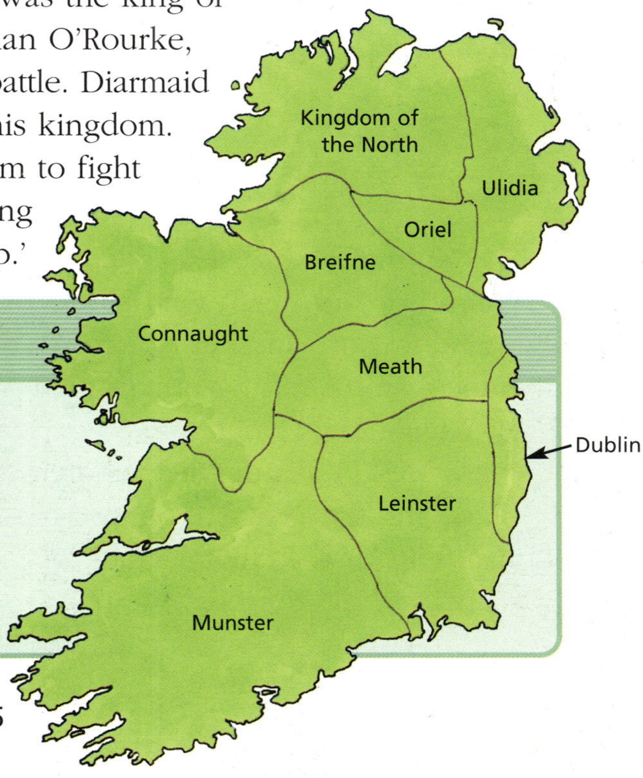

MATTER of FACT

In 1166, Ireland was split into many kingdoms — Munster, Leinster, Connaught, Meath, Dublin, Breifne, Oriel, Ulidia and the Kingdom of the North.

'King Henry II, delighted with this unexpected opportunity to conquer Ireland, sent over his Norman knights.'

'So King Henry sent Strongbow to Ireland?' asked Aoife.

'Yes, eventually. Strongbow was the leader of the Norman knights who arrived in Ireland. He didn't go with them immediately. He first sent an **advance party** of 500 men, led by Robert Fitzstephen. They landed at the port of Bannow in County Wexford on 1 May 1169. They immediately captured Wexford town.'

'My aunt lives in Wexford,' piped up Maureen Fahy.

Aoife smiled. Maureen had aunts in every town in Ireland, it seemed.

'What happened next Mr Harrison?' she asked.

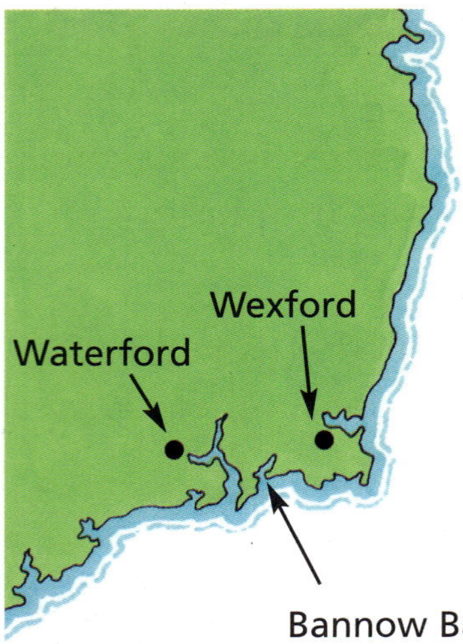

The Normans invaded Ireland from Northern France

MATTER OF FACT

The Normans were descended from Vikings or **Norsemen** who had settled in Normandy in Northern France. In 1066, the Normans, led by William the Conqueror, conquered England. One hundred years later they were about to invade Ireland — by invitation of Diarmaid Mac Murrough!

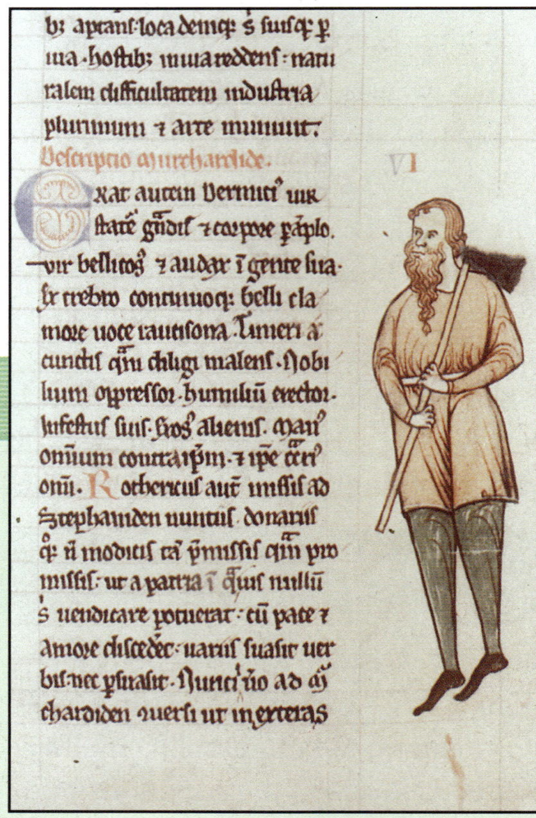

Diarmaid Mac Murrough

Mr Harrison looked at Aoife, bemused. She usually daydreamed through the history class. The tale of Aoife and Strongbow really seemed to have captured her imagination.

'Soon after this, a second Norman force landed in Wexford, at a place called Baginbun. They were led by **Raymond le Gros**.'

'Raymond the Big!' cried Marion, who thought she knew some French. The whole class laughed. Raymond Burke, who was as thin as a whippet, puffed up his cheeks and stuck out his tummy.

'Raymond le Gros at your service,' he grunted.

Mr Harrison looked confused. He waited for the giggling to die down.

'Well, the Irish attacked Raymond le Gros' force of only ten knights and seventy **archers**. Raymond and his men sent a herd of cattle stampeding at his attackers and they managed to overcome the much larger Irish force.'

'Of course we did,' grunted Raymond Burke who enjoyed acting the clown.

'The seventy or so captured Irish soldiers had their arms and legs broken before being thrown off the cliff into the sea where they all drowned. The Normans were not playing games.'

That silenced the class.

'When did Strongbow himself come?' asked Aoife.

'On 23 August 1169,' Mr Harrison replied. 'Strongbow landed at Crook near Waterford with 1 000 men. He joined up with Raymond le Gros and they laid **siege** to Waterford. Waterford held out for only one day before it fell to the Normans.'

Strongbow and Aoife's wedding

'But why did Strongbow marry Aoife in Waterford?' asked Aoife.

'Well,' smiled Mr Harrison, 'this brings us back to the subject of Maclise's painting. In order to persuade Strongbow to come to Ireland, King Diarmaid Mac Murrough had promised Strongbow that he could marry his daughter. Strongbow had fulfilled his side of the bargain so...'

Waterford

'So he handed her over to a complete stranger, like some sort of trophy!' exclaimed Mary indignantly. 'If my Dad ever did that I'd kill him!'

Everyone laughed at that, except Aoife, who did not seem to hear. She was thinking of another Aoife, marrying a complete stranger. A stranger dressed all in armour, among the smoking ruins and the dead and dying of Waterford. What was she thinking? Did she have a choice? Did she learn to love this stranger — or to hate him?

'When Diarmaid Mac Murrough died two years later, his son-in-law, Strongbow, became the new King of Leinster. The Normans were well on their way to taking over the entire country!' Mr Harrison concluded, with a clap of his hands. 'Come on! Now we're going to look at some **Impressionist paintings**!'

With that, Mr Harrison and his lively class headed for the stairs.

MATTER OF FACT

The Bayeux Tapestry is a long narrow tapestry depicting the Norman conquest of England in 1066. It may be seen in the town of Bayeux in Northern France.

MATTER OF FACT

Many more Normans followed Richard de Clare to Ireland. By 1250, just eighty years after Strongbow's arrival, seventy-five per cent of the country was under Norman control.

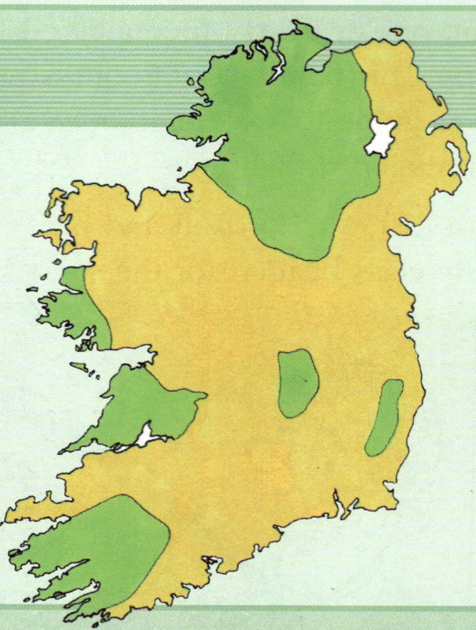

Areas held by native Irish

Areas under Norman control

MATTER OF FACT

Richard de Clare, Strongbow, is buried in Christchurch Cathedral in Dublin. His memorial statue was used for centuries as a place where oaths were sworn by the business people of the city.

Christchurch Cathedral

MATTER OF FACT

Aoife, Strongbow's wife, is buried in the church at Bannow, County Wexford. The city of Bannow itself has largely disappeared. Much of it lies under the water of Bannow Bay while the rest is covered by sand dunes.

MATTER OF FACT

The walled towns of Drogheda, New Ross, Athenry and Galway City were all founded by the Normans.

Galway

MATTER OF FACT

Many Irish people have Norman ancestors. Any surname beginning with the prefix 'fitz' or 'de' is a Norman name: Fitzgerald, Fitzsimon, Fitzpatrick or de Clare, de Lacey or de Vere. Other Norman names include Burke, Lacey, Barry, Prendergast, Cusack, Fleming, Cruise, Plunkett, Nugent, Walshe, Neville and Lambert. You never know … you might be a descendent of Strongbow, Richard de Clare!

Richard de Clare

More Blarney

G

1 Agree or disagree. Support your view with information you have.

- Diarmaid Mac Murrough's actions had no effect on the history of Ireland.
- King Henry II was a kind man to send help to Diarmaid.
- Women were treated with little respect in Norman Times.
- Art galleries and museums are boring places.

P

2 Improvise the conversation you imagine between Princess Aoife and her father when she first discovers that she is part of the bargain he has struck with Strongbow.

Tale and Detail

Choose the correct answers.

	A	B	C	D
The Marriage of Strongbow and Aoife was painted by:	Michelangelo	Daniel Maclise	Raymond Le Gros	Pablo Picasso
Diarmaid's arch-enemy was:	Richard de Clare	Tiernan O'Reilly	Tiernan O'Rourke	King Henry II
Diarmaid promised Aoife's hand in marriage to:	Mr Harrison	King Henry II	Strongbow	Raymond le Gros
The Normans were descendants of:	the Vikings	the Celts	the Welsh	the Egyptians

Work to Discover

Complete the following sentences:

- The Bayeux Tapestry depicts…
- In 1166, Ireland was divided into the kingdoms of…
- The first Normans who landed in the port of Bannow, County Wexford were led by…
- Raymond le Gros overcame the much larger Irish force by…
- Strongbow is buried…
- The *Mona Lisa* can be found in…

Word Wizardry

Synonyms for '**said**':
Synonyms are words with similar meanings.
In this chapter, the following synonyms for the word 'said' are used.

whispered   announced   moaned   exclaimed   grunted

Find each in the text. How do these synonyms improve the story?
Find five more synonyms for 'said' in the text.
Try to use synonyms for 'said' in your next piece of writing.

Surf the Imagination

You are a casting director about to make a film of the book *Strongbow*. Who would you cast in the roles of: Strongbow, Aoife, Diarmaid Mac Murrough, Raymond le Gros, King Henry II? Draw a poster encouraging people to attend the film.

Visual Arts

You are a tour guide in the National Gallery of Ireland. Give a presentation about *The Marriage of Strongbow and Aoife* by Daniel Maclise to a group, using the information you read in this chapter. Have your classmates ask you questions about the painting and its background.

Mouse Search

Read the novel *Strongbow* by Morgan Llewelyn.
Conduct a survey of the surnames of people in your class. How many of them are Norman in origin?
The Bayeux Tapestry depicts the Norman Invasion of England. It also shows **Halley's Comet**. Find out all you can about this phenomenon.
Mark these important dates on a timeline. Using the text, write one sentence about the events of that year:

1066   1166   1169   1854

Final Answer

The Normans came to Ireland at the invitation of:

A William the Conqueror
B The Taoiseach
C Diarmaid Mac Murrough
D Brian Boru

Caves

In C S Lewis' novel, *The Lion, the Witch and the Wardrobe*, Lucy discovers an amazing new world as she explores a house. Although Lucy's world is fictional, enchanting underground worlds have been discovered in real life too. These worlds are called caves and they are sometimes home to rare and beautiful formations.

'I'll kill that silly dog when I find him!' Jessica muttered. Patch, her little terrier, had gone running off after a rabbit — again. She had never been to this part of the hill before. Judging by how overgrown everything was, she doubted anybody else had either. Just then, she heard Patch barking.

Patch seemed to have dug through the soil at the opening of a burrow and squeezed inside it.

Jessica knelt down and looked into the opening. Her heart beat faster when she realised her discovery. This was no burrow, this was a cave! She whooped with joy as she ran down the hill to the picnic area to tell her parents.

As she ran, she began to wonder… how did that cave get there?

Well, it's a little like water dripping onto a concrete path. After a while, the water will create a hole in the concrete. Eventually, the concrete will break up. This is called **erosion**. Caves are formed in the same way — only very, very slowly.

Some rocks are softer than others. A soft rock, such as **limestone**, can be dissolved by rainwater. (Believe it or not, rainwater is a weak acid!) When rain falls on limestone, it eats out tiny holes in the rock. These holes get bigger and bigger. Over many thousands of years, they become tunnels. Water flows through these tunnels and dissolves or **erodes** the rock. Eventually, over millions of years, the tunnels become caves.

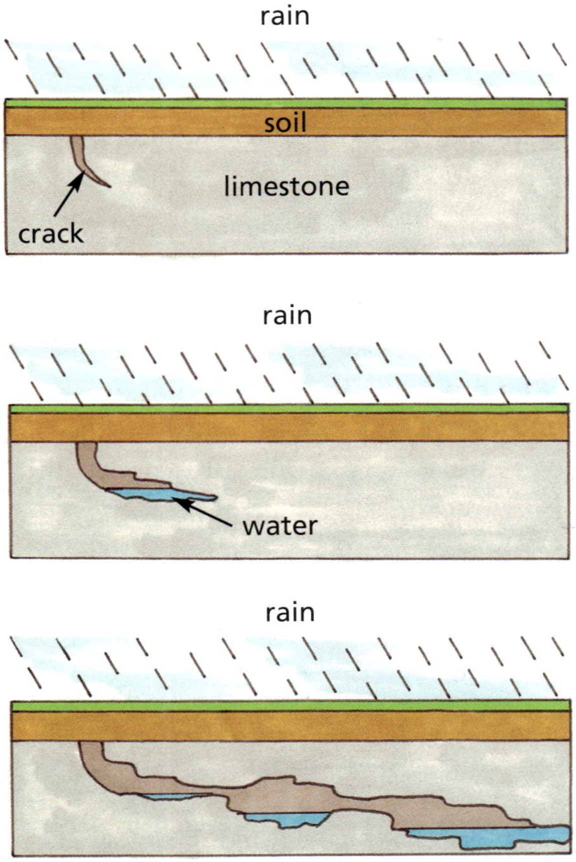

MATTER OF FACT

Often, an entire network of tunnels forms a group of caves. A cave system that still has water flowing through it — an underground river — is called an **active cave system**.

It is hard to imagine, but Ireland was once covered by a warm, shallow sea. Fish of all shapes and sizes darted back and forth in this sea, and the water teemed with tiny microscopic creatures called **plankton**. When this sea life died, their shells and skeletons fell to the seabed. Layer upon layer of these shells and skeletons built up. Each new layer put pressure on the layers below. This pressure caused the layers to **fuse** into rock. This new rock is called limestone.

Over millions of years, the world changed. Ireland is no longer under water. The only clue to that distant past is the soft, grey rock limestone that covers most of the country.

The **Burren** is a large limestone area in the west of Ireland

Water does more than just erode rock. Sometimes it can even build things. How does this happen?

Rainwater sometimes seeps through the ground above a cave. This rainwater can dissolve some of the limestone in the cave roof. This dissolved limestone then drips down from the cave ceiling to the cave floor. Over many, many years this creates special features:

When the drops of dissolved limestone land on the floor and harden, they form **stalagmites**.

When the drops of dissolved limestone harden on the ceiling, they form **stalactites**.

When a stalactite and stalagmite meet and join together, they form a **column**.

stalamites + stalacites only caves have got them stalacites are on the top and mites are on the bott…

stalagmite

stalactite

column

MATTER OF FACT

Straw stalagmites look just like hollow straws that you would use to drink with. They are very **delicate**. It could take hundreds of years for a straw stalagmite to form.

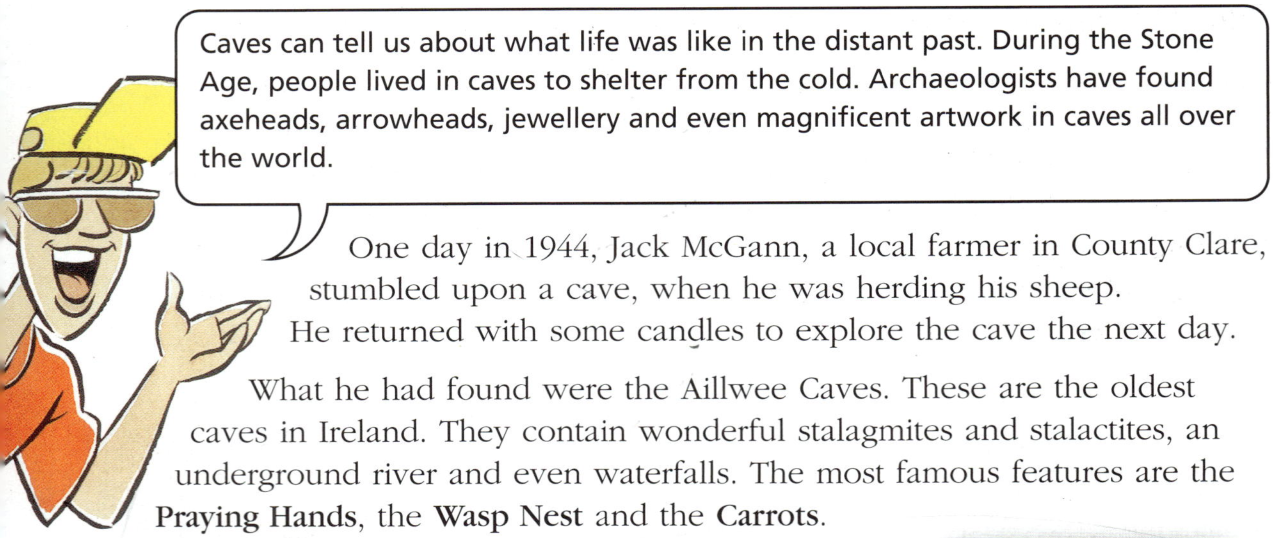

One day in 1944, Jack McGann, a local farmer in County Clare, stumbled upon a cave, when he was herding his sheep. He returned with some candles to explore the cave the next day.

What he had found were the Aillwee Caves. These are the oldest caves in Ireland. They contain wonderful stalagmites and stalactites, an underground river and even waterfalls. The most famous features are the **Praying Hands**, the **Wasp Nest** and the **Carrots**.

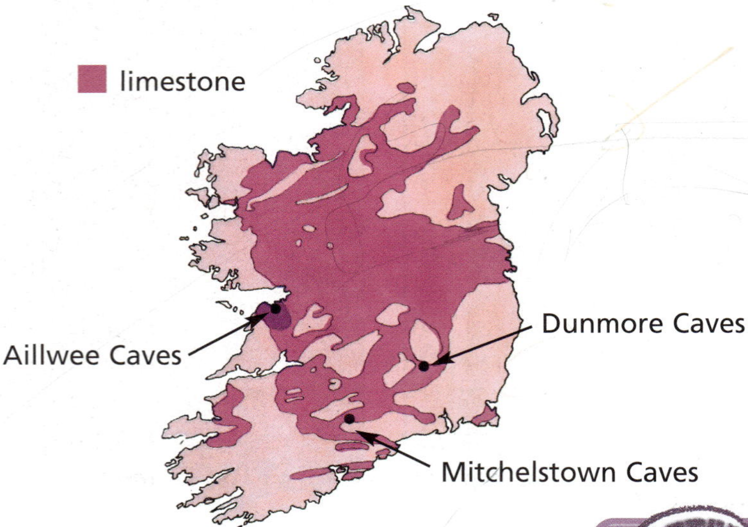

Praying Hands

The caves were **excavated** and opened to the public in 1976. There are daily guided tours of the caves for members of the public.

MATTER OF FACT

Evidence of bears was found in the Aillwee Caves. This proves these animals once lived in Ireland prior to becoming extinct.

MATTER OF FACT

There are several other cave systems in Ireland that are open to the public. These include the Dunmore Caves and the Mitchelstown Caves. A number of these caves also have guided tours that allow people to explore a marvellous **subterranean** world.

The Altamira Cave

One day in 1879, an **amateur archaeologist** called Marcelino de Sautola brought his nine-year-old daughter, Maria, on a day-trip to the Altamira Cave. The Altamira Cave in Northern Spain was famous for its fossils and **artefacts**. As de Sautola busied himself searching for objects on the floor of the cave, Maria glanced up towards the ceiling. The roof was covered with wonderful paintings of horses, deer, **bison** and abstract figures that had lived in Spain during the **Ice Age**. They were painted using vivid blacks, reds and browns. These paintings were at least 15 000 years old.

Cave painting of cattle at Lascaux

Cave painting of bison at Altamira

The Cave at Lascaux

On 12 September 1940, four French schoolboys discovered a **sensational** cave in **Lascaux** in central France. The walls and ceilings were decorated with wonderful paintings of animals and humans. These paintings were more than 17 000 years old. Unfortunately, the paintings became damaged and had to be specially treated by scientists. The cave is no longer open to the public.

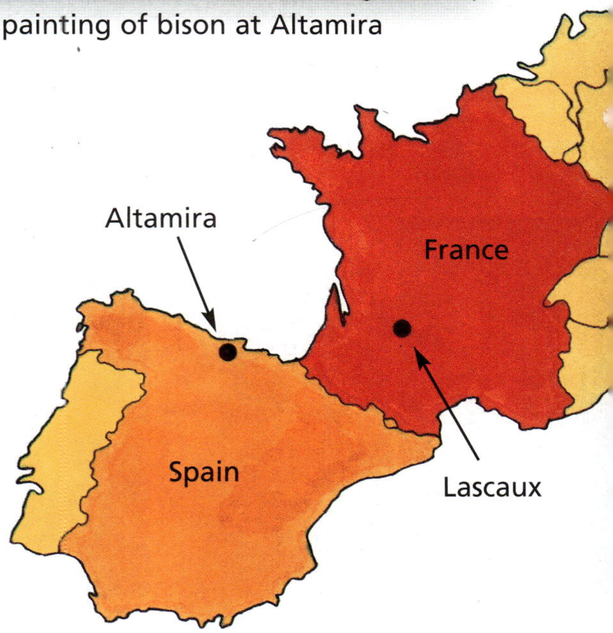

The Seventh Heaven Cave

Dissolved limestone in stalactites and stalagmites can occasionally form beautiful and unusual shapes. Sometimes these rare and beautiful formations are broken off by vandals and kept as souvenirs.

There is one cave, however, where this will never happen. **The Seventh Heaven Cave**, in France, contains the rarest and most exquisite rock crystal formations in the world. The cave is guarded day and night and its exact location is a French state secret.

Very few people are allowed to visit it and those who do, must get permission from the French government. They must wear a blindfold for the journey to and from the cave. They may only remove the blindfolds when they are deep inside the cave itself. They can explore the cave, but only under the strict supervision of their guide! All too soon, they must put their blindfolds on and go back above ground. Anyone who has visited the Seventh Heaven Cave has said it was the 'trip of a lifetime'.

MATTER OF FACT

The longest known **stalactite** is twenty-eight metres long. It was found in a cave in **Brazil** in South America. The tallest known **stalagmite** is even bigger. It is thirty-two metres high! This was found in a cave in **Slovakia** in Eastern Europe.

MATTER OF FACT

There are caves in cliffs by the sea that are formed by waves literally pounding holes in weak points in the cliff rock. There are no features like stalactites and stalagmites in sea caves. This is because cliff rock is not always limestone.

MATTER OF FACT

People who explore caves to study them are called **speleologists**. People who explore caves as a hobby are called **potholers**. The word 'potholing' comes from the word 'pothole', which is the old nickname for a cave. People who go potholing need training, equipment and courage! It can be a dangerous pastime. Sometimes the caves can be very deep and the tunnels very narrow. Potholers may have to **wade** through underground rivers. This water is always very cold because it gets no sunlight.

Experts believe that there are many large cave systems under the midlands of Ireland (an area which is largely made up of limestone). Who knows? Maybe Jessica found another 'Seventh Heaven'?

More Blarney

1 Agree or disagree. Support your view with information you have.
- When drops of limestone harden on the ceilings of caves, they form stalagmites.
- The paintings in the Lascaux Cave are over 17 000 years old.
- Evidence of dinosaurs has been found in the Aillwee Caves.
- The Seventh Heaven Cave in France is open to the public.

2 Anyone who has visited the Seventh Heaven Cave in France has said that it was the 'trip of a lifetime'. What, for you, was, or would be, the trip of a lifetime?

Tale and Detail

Complete the sentences. Write the answers in your copybook.

	A	B	C	D
Where is the Burren?	Spain	Ireland	Australia	France
What rock covers most of Ireland?	granite	marble	limestone	concrete
What forms when stalagmites and stalactites meet?	pillars	columns	waterfalls	potholes
What did farmer Jack McGann discover?	The Lascaux Cave	The Altamira Cave	The Aillwee Caves	The Mitchelstown Caves
What is potholing?	exploring caves	exploring oceans	rock-climbing	repairing roads

Work to Discover

Look at the table.
Find the photographs listed.
Write three sentences about each photograph.

Photograph	Page
the Burren	16
a column	17
cave paintings at Lascaux	19
potholers	21

Word Wizardry

Word Fun - Nicknames

A **pothole** was an old nickname for a cave.
Make up nicknames for the following:

mountain	**river**	**cliff**	**volcano**	**earthquake**
thunderstorm	**lightning**	**avalanche**	**tidal wave**	**hurricane**

Making Words

Make as many words as you can from the letters of the word **stalagmite**.

Surf the Imagination

1 Make your own cave painting that you would like people to discover thousands of years from now.
2 Imagine you are on holidays in the midlands of Ireland when you come across an **Eighth Heaven**! Write the story of your discovery.

Mouse Search

1 Do a project on a cave in your own locality or on one of the caves you read about in this chapter. Include photographs or your own sketches.
2 Find out all you can about the Mitchelstown Caves and the Dunmore Caves.
3 Find out about exotic flowers that grow in the Burren in County Clare.
4 Why is the water in caves so cold? Find out about the sun as a source of energy and heat.

Final Answer

What name is given to a person who explores caves to study them?

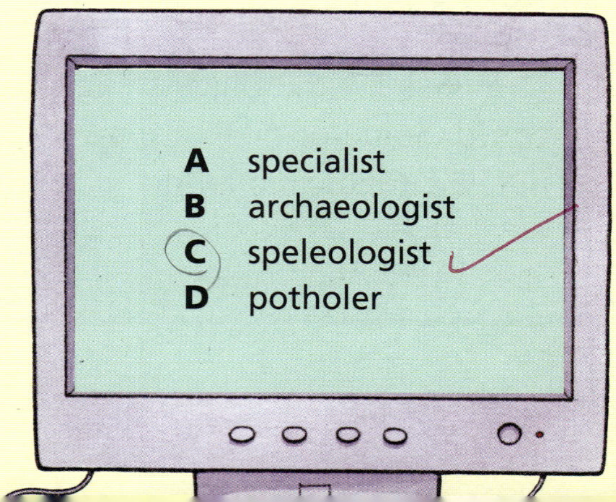

A specialist
B archaeologist
C speleologist
D potholer

Animal magic

In the novel, *The Borrowers*, by Mary Norton, both Arrietty and 'the boy' think that they have met a magical creature. There are many creatures in the world that seem magical to us. This is because they have found amazing ways of doing things.

Getting a good start

Human babies need a lot of care and attention. When they are very small, they are fed, clothed, walked, changed and protected almost every minute of the day. The young of some animals, such as turtles, have to fend for themselves as soon as they are born. Most of them do not survive into adulthood.

A turtle

Emperor penguins

The parents of other creatures, however, make more of an effort to help their young to grow and develop! A male **emperor penguin** will stand in temperatures as low as -18° Celcius with a single egg balanced on his feet for more than two months. The female, meanwhile, hunts fish for the chick that will hatch from the egg. The male ostrich also minds the eggs. He will sit on up to thirty eggs, which have been laid by several females.

MATTER OF FACT

Ostriches lay the biggest eggs in the world. Some of them are up to fifteen centimetres long.

Feeding times

One of the most important tricks in the animal world is to avoid becoming lunch for something else. In the sea, about ninety per cent of all creatures end up as food for predators. An adult blue whale will eat about five tonnes of food (mostly **krill** — a kind of tiny shrimp) every day. The shark has been described as the perfect predator. Sharks may have as many as 3 000 teeth in their mouths at any one time.

A shark

A mosquito

The female **anopheles mosquito** feeds on human blood. It only takes a small bite from its victims, but the mosquitoes often carry the **malaria parasite**. This enters the victim's blood and causes the malaria disease. A half of all the human deaths that have ever happened, about twenty-six billion, have been caused by malaria.

MATTER OF FACT

Some animals just eat and eat. A horse needs to graze for twenty hours every day. It only sleeps for four hours a day.

Getting about

Some animals travel huge distances at high speeds, while others take life at a slower pace. A swift flies 1 000 kilometres in one day when hunting for insects. An arctic tern, however, will travel a distance of about 36 000 kilometres in one year. On the other hand, the three-toed sloth only manages to go about 100 metres in an hour. It could only travel about three kilometres in a day, even if it kept moving all the time.

An artic tern

A three-toed sloth

Sometimes, knowing where you are going is more important than how far you can travel. Bats are well known for using **echolocation** for hunting prey and for finding their way about. Their high-pitched squeaks and clicks bounce off objects and echo back to the bats' ears. This helps them, not only to determine where a thing is, but also *what* it is. Some bats have such sensitive echolocation that they can detect a single human hair from one metre away.

A bat

MATTER OF FACT

The sooty tern can fly for four years without landing. It feeds and sleeps 'on the wing' and will land only to mate and to lay eggs.

Home sweet home

Most birds build nests out of twigs and feathers. Others prefer a sturdier structure! Swallows mix mud with grass and build their nests in the **eaves** of houses. The swallows fly for thousands of miles and still return to the same nest, year after year. The nests usually need only a few small repairs.

Swallows

Wasps build their nests by chewing wood and turning it into a material like paper. They use this as a building material. Other wasps build with mud. These are called **potter wasps**.

A wasp

The most amazing animal builders are termites. Termites use mud to make a type of cement. Using this 'cement', they build complicated termite hills. These hills are organised into separate 'zones' such as food stores, a nursery for the **larvae** or grubs and royal chambers where the queen lays her eggs. A queen termite may lay 30 000 eggs a day for several months. The entire structure is maintained at the right temperature by a complicated system of chimneys and air vents. You could say termites invented air conditioning long before we did!

Termite hills can reach six metres in height and house a colony of millions of termites

Head lice love clean human hair. Lice grasp hair with a single claw on each of their feet. These claws are amazingly powerful. A **louse** can resist a pull of one kilogramme! Lice lay eggs called **nits**, which they glue to your hair. A single louse can lay about 300 eggs over six weeks. Lice may be easily removed with medicine from the chemist.

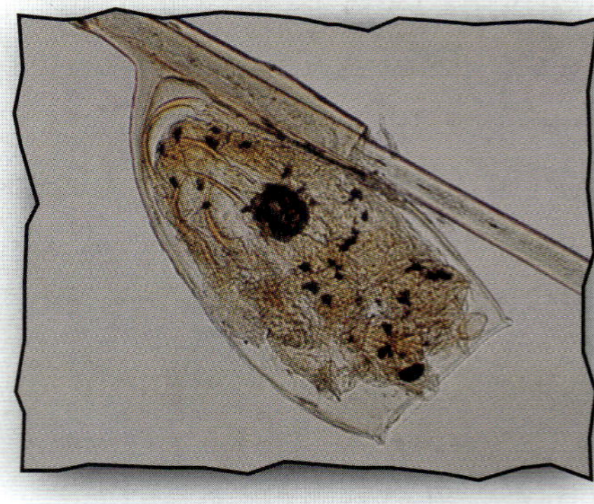

A lice nit on hair

Another common parasite is the flea. Fleas can jump over two hundred times their own length. They like to hop from one human **host** to another. Fleas bite through your skin to suck your blood. Back in the Middle Ages, fleas, carried by rats and mice, spread the disease called the Black Death. This caused about twenty-five million deaths.

A mouse

MATTER of FACT

Skin parasites are also a common problem for large animals. Ticks, mites and lice are very difficult for an animal like the elephant to remove. The **African cattle egret** lands on the backs of large animals and picks out the parasites with its beak. The bird gets an easy meal and the herd animal gets rid of some troublesome pests.

An egret

Smart animals — who is the cleverest of them all?

Chimpanzees

We humans consider ourselves to be the most intelligent species on the planet, but there are close contenders in the animal world. Humans and chimpanzees have many common features. Like humans, chimpanzees are able to make and to use tools. They organise themselves into family groups and plan and carry out sophisticated hunting raids on other animals. Chimpanzees and gorillas cannot speak like us because of the structure of their throats, but they communicate using voice and facial gestures. Some chimpanzees know more than 200 signs.

At sea, **cetaceans** (dolphins, porpoises and whales) have their own special languages that they use to communicate with one another. Each species has its own language, made up of whistles, clicks and songs. Sound travels about four times better through water than it does through air. Cetaceans of the same species can communicate with one another over distances of hundreds of kilometres.

A dolphin

MATTER OF FACT

The call of the humpback whale is the loudest noise made by a living creature. Its call is louder than a large jet taking off. It is believed that one humpback can hear another's call from a distance of over 320 kilometres.

Humpback whales

Living to a ripe old age

Most animals have ways of ensuring that they will live to a ripe old age. Bright colours, such as red and yellow, are common danger signals to insects and frogs. Some **exotic** species of frog hold powerful poison in their skin. They are brightly coloured to warn would-be predators — 'We don't taste nice!' Many insects do exactly the same thing. Wasps use their black and yellow marking as a danger warning.

Other animals are experts in **camouflage**. Butterflies look like leaves. **Stick insects** look like withered twigs. Even a large animal like the zebra will use its bold pattern of stripes. In the shimmering heat of the African plains, it is difficult to tell one zebra from another when they stand together.

Of course, a lot of the predators use camouflage to capture their prey

MATTER OF FACT

Chemicals made in the skin of some poison dart frogs of South America are the deadliest of all natural poisons. They can kill a person in less than a minute.

MATTER OF FACT

Horses, elephants, cattle and deer may all sleep standing up.

MATTER OF FACT

Locusts travel in swarms that can cover up to 250 square kilometres and may contain tens of millions of individual locusts. The biggest recorded swarm had over forty billion insects!

MATTER OF FACT

If you try to catch a lizard by the tail, the animal will allow its tail to break off so that it may escape. In time, the lizard will grow another new tail. This trick is called **auto amputation**.

MATTER OF FACT

Hummingbirds may not travel long distances but they have to beat their wings up to 5 400 times a minute in order to hover in front of flowers to drink their nectar.

More Blarney

1 Agree or disagree. Support your view with information you have.
- Animals have been responsible for millions of human deaths.
- Chimpanzees are by far the most intelligent mammals.
- The mosquito is a harmless creature.
- Animals can communicate with each other.

2 Discuss with your partner or group what you consider to be the five most interesting facts about animals that you read in this chapter.

Tale and Detail

1 How does the male emperor penguin help its young?
2 What is one of the most important 'tricks' in the animal world?
3 Why is the shark described as the perfect predator?
4 How do bats hunt their prey and find their way about?
5 How did the Black Death spread in the Middle Ages?
6 What is the biggest recorded swarm of locusts?

Work to Discover

Name It!

1 It feeds on human blood and often carries the malaria parasite.
2 It lays the biggest eggs in the world.
3 It can fly for four years without landing.
4 It grazes for twenty hours and eats for four hours per day.
5 It beats its wings about 5 400 times a minute to hover in front of flowers.
6 Its call is the loudest noise made by a living creature.
7 It travels at a speed of 100 metres an hour.
8 It lands on the backs of large animals and picks out parasites with its beak.

Word Wizardry

Collective Nouns

Match the collective noun with the animal.

A swarm of	locusts
A herd of	whales
A gaggle of	bats
A school of	geese
A colony of	swallows
A troop	monkeys
A plague of	elephants
A flight of	bees

Make a chart of collective nouns and add more as you find them.

Idioms

It is said that 'Nature is red in tooth and claw'.
What do you think this means?

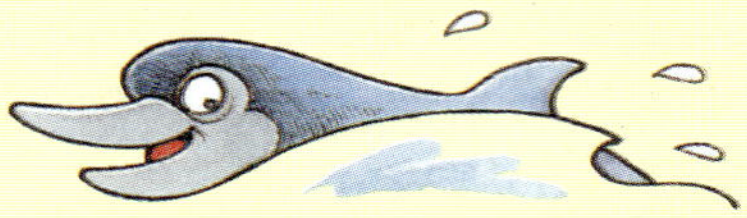

Surf the Imagination

Many fictitious characters have been given the features and abilities of animals e.g. Batman and Spiderman. Make up your own character and create a comic strip to recount one of his or her adventures.

In his Just So stories, Rudyard Kipling invents stories to explain 'How the Leopard Got His Spots' and 'How the Rhinoceros Got His Skin'. Write a story telling how one of the animals you read about in this chapter came to be 'just so'.

Imagine you have discovered a new species of animal. Describe its appearance, habitat and diet. Name and illustrate your discovery.

Mouse Search

Find five facts about an animal you are curious to learn more about.

Find out how echolocation, used by bats, and radar, used by ships and aircraft, are similar.

Final Answer

About half of all human deaths that happened were caused by:

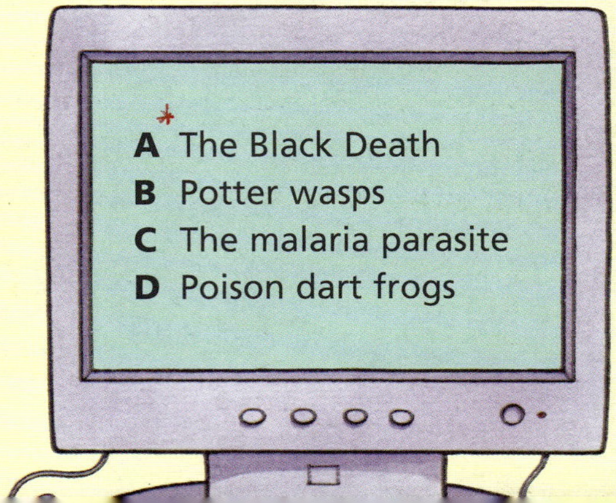

Bogs

In *The Sea Wall*, by Eilís Dillon, Sally is frightened by the awesome power of the sea. Nature can be very destructive, but it can also provide use with many resources. One of Ireland's most important natural resources are our bogs.

Thanks to the enthusiasm of Ms Fortune, the fifth class were really looking forward to their school trip to 'Explore an Irish Bog'. All except Nicholas. Nicholas dreaded exploring an Irish bog because he knew who the tour guide would be. Uncle Stephen! It was not that he did not like his Uncle Stephen — quite the opposite. He just did not trust his uncle to behave himself in front of his school friends. Nicholas was shy by nature — and Uncle Stephen was not!

Nicholas was the last to get off the bus. He tried to make himself as **unobtrusive** as possible. Needless to say, Uncle Stephen spotted him straightaway.

'That's my nephew, Nicholas, trying to hide!' he bellowed out. Everyone turned to look at Nicholas.

'Hi Uncle Stephen,' Nicholas mumbled, his ears reddening.

Uncle Stephen was dressed in a large yellow **oilskin** and big dirty boots. In one hand he held a peculiar looking spade.

'Follow me,' he called out and walked off into the bog. The class went trotting and stumbling after him. After a while, Uncle Stephen stopped and turned.

'Soggy, isn't it?' he bellowed.

'Yes,' agreed Siobhán, who had stepped into a deep hole. She was leaning on Ms Fortune's shoulder while she poured brown water out of her boots. Uncle Stephen threw back his head and laughed.

'What else do you notice about the ground?' he shouted out.

'It's very bouncy,' chipped in Peter.

'Clever boy!' boomed Uncle Stephen as he started jumping up and down. Soon the whole class was moving up and down. Even if you stood still the jumping of the children around you made the ground move.

'In winter, a bog is heavy and wet,' explained Uncle Stephen when the jumping had stopped, 'but in the summer it gets light and dry. Early in the summer you get the best of both worlds. You still have to watch out for **bog holes**, though!'

'Is that what I stepped into?' asked Siobhán.

'Yes, but they can be a lot deeper than the one you found. You were lucky, although your socks were not!' He laughed and clapped his hands.

'Now we are going to dig some turf. Does anyone know what this is called?' he asked, holding up an odd looking spade with a two-sided blade.

'A **sleán**,' answered Emer.

'Brilliant!' joked Uncle Stephen, and Emer smiled.

Nicholas was beginning to relax a little.

'Your uncle is alright,' whispered Karl. Nicholas smiled.

'Turf is a **fossil fuel**,' his Uncle Stephen continued. 'In the old days, entire families would head off to the bog on a fine day. They would cut large rectangular-shaped sods of turf with sleáns like this one. They tossed the sods up into long rows on the ground and left them to dry. It was heavy work and required great skill. If you look here, you can see a **drill** where the turf has been cut.' Uncle Stephen pointed out a cut away section of the bog.

'Of course, nowadays the sleán is rarely used. People use large machines to cut turf.'

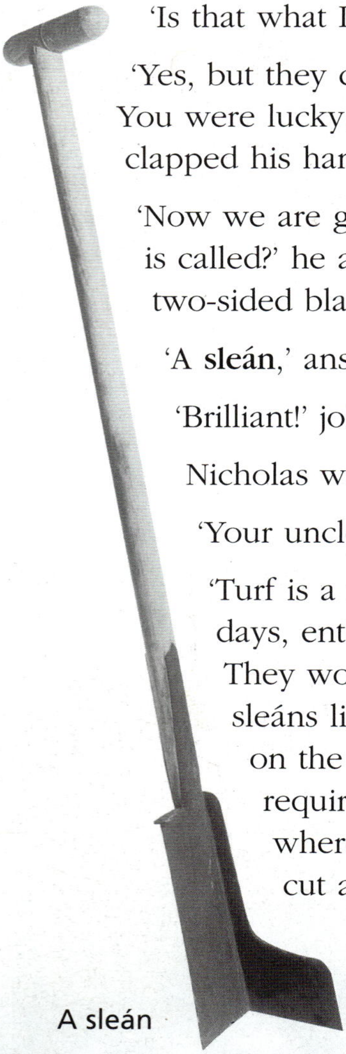

A sleán

A turf-cutting machine at work in a bog

'When the sods of turf were dry, they were stacked into little pyramids called **footings**. In the late summer or early autumn, the sods were collected into baskets called **creels**. The sods were then stacked beside the house and used as fuel for the winter.'

Stacking sods of turf into footings

'Who would like to try and use the sleán?'

Of course, everyone had a go but only a few children could manage it. Nicholas was, in fact, the best of them.

'That's my nephew!' roared out Uncle Stephen and clapped him on the back, nearly knocking him over.

'Is that how **Bord na Mona** makes briquettes?' asked Orla.

'Not exactly, no.' Uncle Stephen smiled at Orla. 'Bord na Mona have huge machines for **milling**. This means turning the top layer of the bog into powder. The 'milled' peat is sprayed out of the back of the machine. It is spread out in a layer over the bog. When it dries, most of it is brought to **power stations** where it is burned to generate electricity. The powder is also sold as **peat moss** and used in our gardens. What's left is **compressed** into the briquettes that Orla burns in her fire!'

Sods of turf in a basket

'Bord na Mona does most of its work on **raised bogs** in the Midlands.'

'Is this a raised bog?' asked Peter.

'No,' said Uncle Stephen. 'This is a **blanket bog**.'

'What's the difference?' asked Peter again.

'There's always one who asks the hard questions!' laughed Uncle Stephen and winked at Ms Fortune. Nicholas wished he would not do that, but Ms Fortune just gave Uncle Stephen a grin. She did not seem to mind.

'Well,' he began, 'peat, or turf, began to form in Ireland about 10 000 years ago, after the last Ice Age. When the Ice Age was over, the climate got warmer and the ice began to melt. Shallow lakes formed all over central Ireland. Are you with me?'

'Yes,' chorused the class.

'**Pondweed** and **water lilies** floated on these lakes and reeds grew around the edges. When these plants died — as they do — they floated to the bottom of the lakes and **decomposed** very slowly. Over years and years, the plant remains built up on the bed of the lakes, forming a layer of peat. Are you still with me?'

They were.

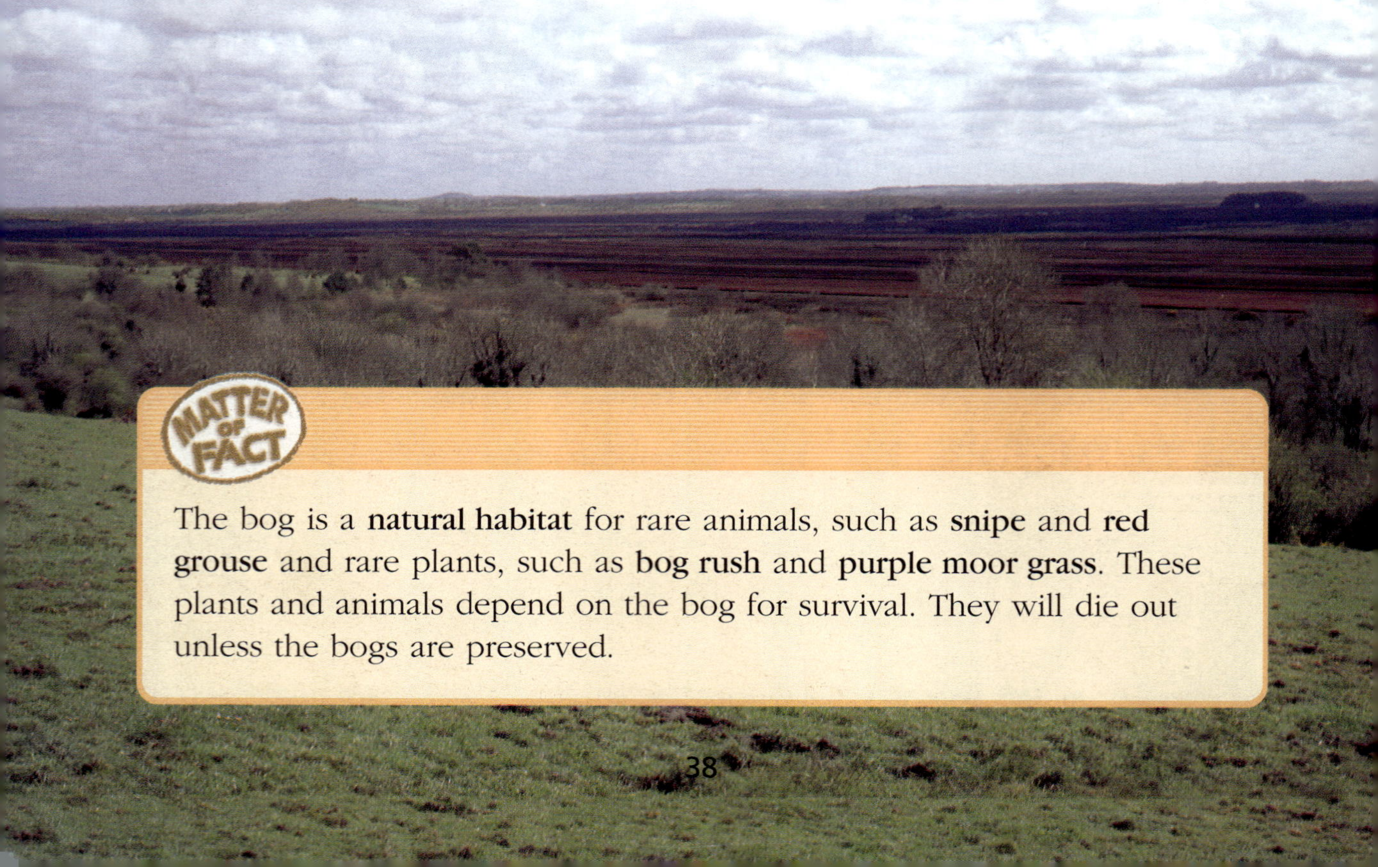

MATTER OF FACT

The bog is a **natural habitat** for rare animals, such as **snipe** and **red grouse** and rare plants, such as **bog rush** and **purple moor grass**. These plants and animals depend on the bog for survival. They will die out unless the bogs are preserved.

Pollardstown Fen

'Over thousands of years, this peat layer becomes thicker and thicker — like me!' chuckled Uncle Stephen and patted his ample tummy. 'This gradually raises the level of the water in the lakes. Now here's what you need to remember. Peat which forms below the water level is called **fen peat**. The largest fen in Ireland is the Pollardstown Fen in County Kildare.'

Uncle Stephen paused for a moment and then addressed himself to Peter.

'However, Peter, to answer your question, given the right conditions, peat keeps on growing. Eventually the layer of peat becomes so thick that it fills the lake entirely and grows up over the top. This is called a raised bog. Did you follow all that?'

'Yes, but what about the blanket bogs? How are they formed?' Peter insisted.

The class groaned and Uncle Stephen put his two big hands around Peter's neck and pretended to strangle him.

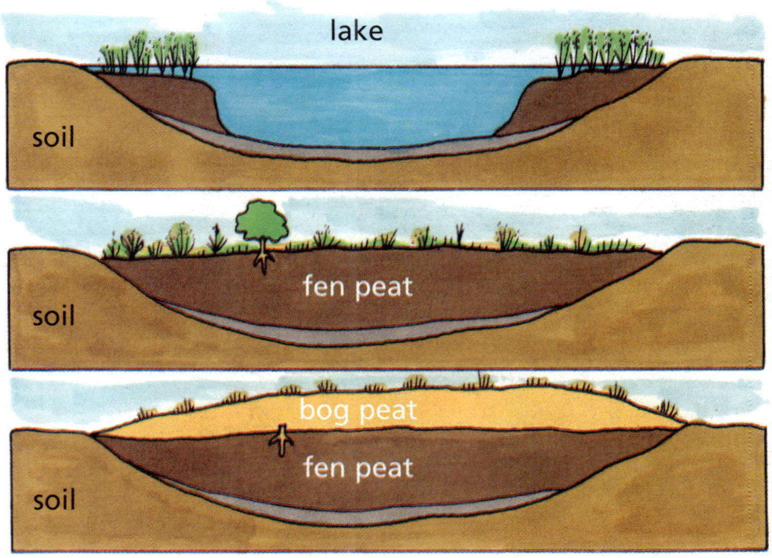

Formation of a raised bog

'Right. Blanket bogs are found mostly in the West of Ireland. As you well know, it rains a lot there! This rain washes minerals like iron down through the soil. Eventually these minerals collect and form a waterproof barrier called an **Iron Pan**. It is like the bottom of a metal basin down there under the bog.' Uncle Stephen stamped his foot on the bog. 'No water can get through and so the ground gets water-logged and — '

' — peat begins to form!' Peter finished off the sentence. Uncle Stephen grinned and ruffled Peter's hair.

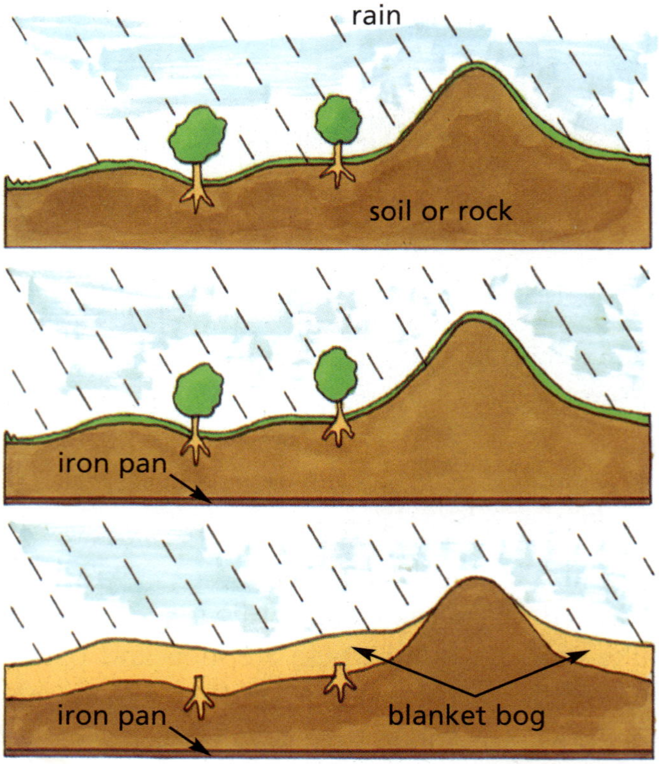

Formation of a blanket bog

Excavating a bog body

'Good man, Peter,' he praised him. 'There are **lowland blanket bogs** like this one and **mountain blanket bogs** like that one over there,' and the class looked across at the mountain Uncle Stephen was pointing to.

'Any more questions?'

'They have found bodies in bogs, haven't they?' piped up Elizabeth. Now that's what Nicholas considered a good question!

'They have indeed! They found a body not far from here. You can see it in the National Museum. There are many natural chemicals in bogs that help **preserve** things, so the body is in excellent condition. It is wearing a hooded cloak and tunic. It was probably a human sacrifice. These were sometimes made to please the gods and goddesses whom people believed had been banished to the **Underworld**.' Uncle Stephen paused for effect. 'In fact, some of the bodies that have been found in bogs are of people who were obviously buried alive.'

Meenybradden bog body

Uncle Stephen then clapped his hands loudly and declared that he was starving.

'Time for lunch,' he announced. 'After you lot have had a short break we are going for a walk across the bog to see what flowers we can find. Keep your eyes out for any unusual birds!'

With that, the class pulled out their lunch boxes and erupted into noisy conversation. Uncle Stephen grinned at Nicholas and stole two of his ham sandwiches. Together they set off over the bog with the rest of the class.

More Blarney

G

1 Agree or disagree. Support your view with information you have.
- Bogs are dry places to visit.
- Bodies found in bogs are badly decomposed.
- Failure to preserve bogs could lead to the extinction of some species of birds and animals.

P

2 Explain to your partner, in your own words, the difference between a raised bog and a blanket bog.

Tale and Detail

Complete the sentences. Write the answers in your copybook.

	A	B	C	D
A sleán is	a basket	a fossil fuel	a ball	a spade with a two-sided blade
Footings are	baskets	boots worn while cutting turf	stacks of dry turf	bog holes
The largest fen in Ireland is in	County Kilkenny	County Offaly	County Kildare	County Wicklow
Most milled peat is brought to	the National Museum	Uncle Stephen's house	garden centres	power stations

Work to Discover

1 When did peat and turf begin to form in Ireland?
2 What is fen peat?
3 Where in Ireland are most blanket bogs found?
4 Why were people buried in bogs?

Word Wizardry

Opposites

In the story, Nicholas tries to make himself as **unobtrusive** as possible. The opposites of certain words can be formed by adding the prefix **un**, **in** or **im**. Write the opposites of the following words:

visible	**comfortable**	**correct**	**pleasant**	**possible**
wise	**perfect**	**convenient**	**secure**	**complete**
able	**sufficient**	**patient**	**conscious**	**direct**

Surf the Imagination

1 While out cutting turf, you discover a bog body. Write the story of what happened.
2 Look at the photos of bogs in this chapter. Paint a copy of one of them.

Mouse Search

1 Turf is a fossil fuel – a non-renewable form of energy. Find out about renewable sources of energy (e.g. wind and sun).
2 Bord na Mona is responsible for monitoring Irish bogs. Find out about the areas of responsibility of each of the following. If possible, visit their websites.

Bord Fáilte	**An Bord Bainne**
Bord Glas	**Bord Altranais**

3 Write or e-mail ENFO requesting information on Ireland's bogs.

Final Answer

The Iron Pan is:

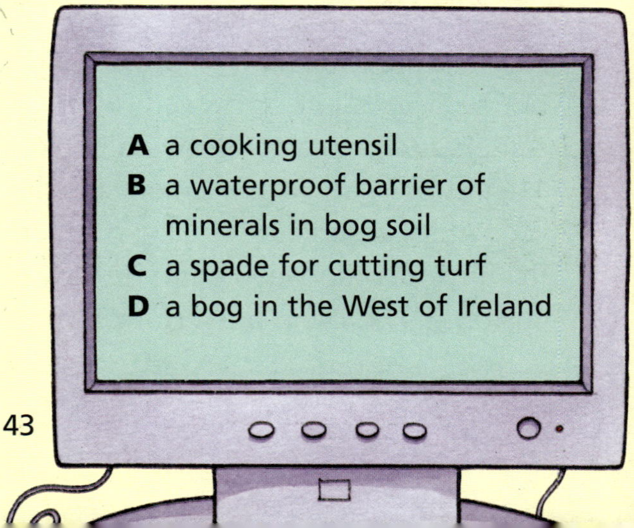

Native Americans

In the novel, *Street Child*, Berlie Doherty writes about poor people who are left in a workhouse and forgotten about. There are many 'forgotten' people in the history of the world. One such people are the Native Americans.

It was Seán who suggested that they visit the **Native American reserve**. His family were on holidays in North Dakota in America. Sean had always been fascinated by **American Indians**. Now he would see them at first hand!

Their guide was a **Native American**. She was dressed in **traditional** clothes and wore **deerskin moccasins** on her feet. As she showed the visitors around, she explained that the first Native Americans arrived about 12 000 years ago. Their **descendants** spread out over the entire country and up into at least 300 tribes, speaking up to 200 languages.

MATTER OF FACT

Native Americans believed that land was sacred. To them, land could not be fenced off or owned. In the 19th century, white European settlers tried to take all the valuable farming land for themselves. They drove the Native Americans onto special areas called **reserves** (i.e. areas 'reserved' for Native American use). Unfortunately, this unwelcome way of life destroyed the Native American culture and customs. The once powerful tribes have since largely died out.

The guide explained that she was **Sioux**. The Sioux was one of the biggest of the Native American tribes. When she showed them pictures of the great Sioux leaders, **Sitting Bull** and **Crazy Horse**, the guide spoke with great pride in her voice. However, as Seán looked around him at the reservation where the descendants of these great warriors now lived, he felt sad. How could such a great people and their culture be reduced to little more than a tourist attraction?

In the craft shop they visited before leaving the reservation, Seán bought himself a book and a small bow and arrow. As he left the shop, he walked past an old Indian who was standing very still and staring ahead expressionlessly. He was dressed in full **ceremonial** dress and held a long, decorated **lance** by his side. As Seán left the shop, to his great surprise, the Indian lifted his hand and pulled out an eagle feather from his head-dress. He handed this to Seán without saying a word.

MATTER OF FACT

'Sioux' was actually the European name for the tribe. The original name was **Dakota**. The Sioux was one of the many tribes of **Plains Indians**. These tribes lived and hunted on the Great Plains region, a grassy area that stretched for 3 200 kilometres between the Rocky Mountains and the Mississippi River.

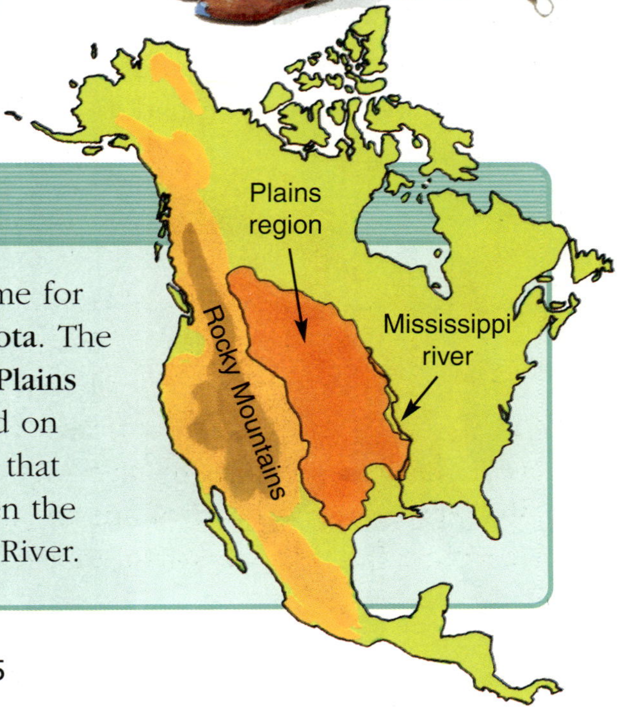

That night, Seán put the eagle feather under his pillow. He fell asleep and had a strange dream. In his dream he was an eagle, soaring high above the Great Plains of North America.

From a height, he could see a huge herd of buffalo on a plain. There seemed to be thousands of them. Far below him, there was a Sioux Indian, wearing a wolf's skin. He was creeping up on a lone buffalo. Seán watched as the Sioux raised his bow. With a single arrow, the Sioux Indian shot the buffalo in the neck and killed it.

Seán flew on and soon found a group of Sioux Indians setting up camp. He hovered overhead, watching two Sioux women putting up a **tepee**. First they tied long poles together to make a cone. Then they covered the cone with buffalo hides which had been sewn together. The skins were decorated with paintings of buffalo and other animals. The tepee even had a smoke flap.

A tepee

The Sioux depended on buffalo for food, clothes and shelter

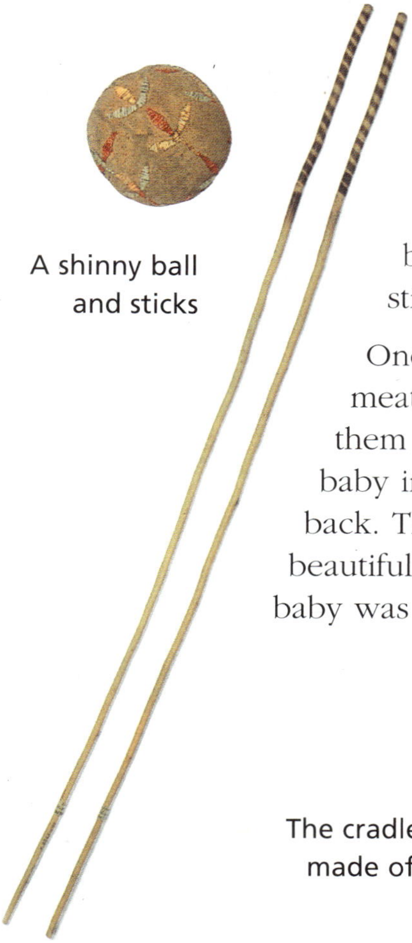

A shinny ball
and sticks

There was an air of contentment and friendliness about the camp. A young boy was being shown how to use a bow and arrow by his father. Some children were playing a ball game called '**shinny**'. The ball was made out of buffalo hide. The children were using long, curved sticks to get the ball past each other's goalposts.

One woman was cutting buffalo meat into strips, and hanging them out to dry. She had a baby in a **cradleboard** on her back. The cradleboard was beautifully decorated and the baby was gurgling happily.

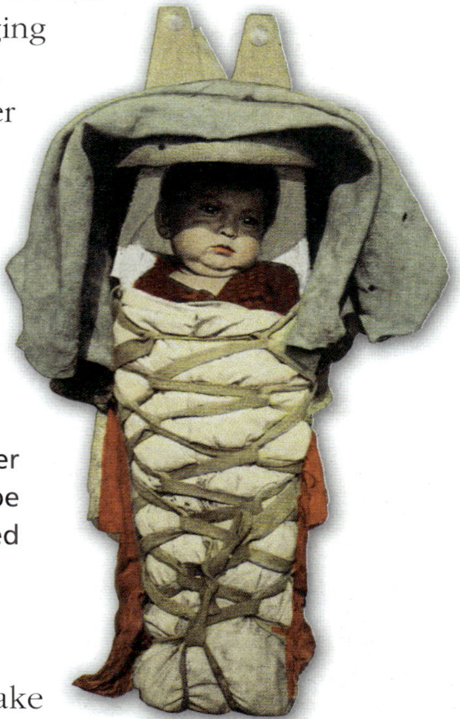

The cradleboard was a baby-carrier made of buffalo skins. It could be laced tightly closed

Other Sioux were busy mixing dry buffalo meat with fat and berries. Seán guessed this was to make **pemmican**. Pemmican was a nutritious food that could be stored for months. It would be used in winter when food was scarce. Seán watched as the Sioux stored the pemmican in large pouches called parfleches.

When Seán awoke, he could remember every detail of his dream. The Eagle feather was still beneath his pillow. He left it there. The next night he also had a strange dream.

parfleche

In the second dream, Seán was again an eagle. He hovered high above the plains and watched a great buffalo herd thundering by beneath him. Many Sioux hunters galloped along on horseback behind them. Some were riding bareback, others were using saddles.

Each hunter wore **quivers** of arrows on their backs. They were shooting at the buffalo from close range. Seán could hear their whoops of excitement, even above the thunder of buffalo hooves. When the Sioux hunters killed a buffalo, they cut out the animal's tongue. This was eaten as a **delicacy**.

Many Sioux used saddles made of **tanned hide** which had been stuffed with buffalo hair

MATTER OF FACT

Spanish settlers brought trained horses to America in 1541. The Plains Indians began to hunt on horseback, moving faster and killing more buffalo. A huge number of buffalo were slaughtered by both Native Americans and Europeans. In 1800, there were over sixty million buffalo on the Great Plains of North America. By 1850, there were only twenty million buffalo. By 1889, only 541 buffalo remained. Their reduced numbers meant the end of the way of life for the Plains Indians.

Seán flew on and saw more Sioux **bartering** with settlers from the 'old world' (Europe). The Europeans were trading kettles, pots, knives, mirrors, beads, guns and whisky. In exchange, the Sioux were trading animal skins and furs.

Once again, Seán flew over a camp. This time a young girl was being buried. She had died from the measles. Her body had been wrapped in buffalo skin and was being placed on a high platform where animals could not get it. Her family stood around in mourning.

A Native American burial

MATTER OF FACT

Europeans brought many new diseases with them. Almost one million Native Americans died of smallpox and measles — diseases against which they had no defence.

Seán knew that Plains Indians believed that dead people went to the spirit world. The spirit world was everywhere — in plants, animals and people. The most powerful spirits, the **Thunderbirds**, ruled the Upper World, which was a world above the sky. Seán watched as Wapiya, the medicine man, performed a healing ceremony for another sick child.

Seán awoke feeling **melancholy**. The feather was still underneath his pillow. With mixed feelings he decided to leave it there.

A medicine man performing a healing ceremony

In his third dream, Seán saw very few buffalo. Instead, he saw European settlers pushing farther and farther west. The Government was driving the Native Americans from their lands and fencing off the once open plains. Seán watched sadly as Sioux tribes were led onto a reservation by the warrior **Red Cloud**.

However, others fought back. In 1876, when the Government demanded to buy Black Hills from the Sioux, **Sitting Bull** and **Crazy Horse** were outraged. Black Hills was sacred Sioux territory. The warriors led the Sioux Indians into battle and they defeated the Government army (led by General Custer) in the bloody Battle of the Little Bighorn. However, more and more Government soldiers arrived, and the winter following was long and hungry for the Sioux. Sitting Bull fled, with his people, to Canada. Crazy Horse, unable to watch his people die of hunger, reluctantly led them onto the reservation.

A re-enactment of the Battle of the Little Bighorn

As Seán flew by, he finally understood what had become of a once great people and their culture. In the morning, when he awoke, the eagle feather was gone.

MATTER OF FACT

1n 1838, thousands of **Cherokee** Indians were driven off their lands by white settlers who were looking for gold. The Cherokee were forced to leave their villages, their burial places and their hunting grounds and to march west. Their journey was called the **Trail of Tears**. About 4 000 people died of cold, starvation and disease as they walked 1 000 kilometres through swamps, rivers, forests, mountains, snow and ice to their new 'home' in Oklahoma.

MATTER OF FACT

In 1847, the **Choctaw** tribe collected $70 (equivalent to $5 000 in today's money) for the victims of famine in Ireland. This was a great act of generosity from a people who had such troubles of their own.

MATTER OF FACT

Geronimo (1829-1909) was the most famous warrior of the Apache tribe. This was a tribe of hunters and warriors who lived in the **arid** mountains and deserts of Southwest America. Geronimo's Apache name was **Goyanthlay**, which meant 'the yawner'. Geronimo fought the Americans who were invading Apache lands in the 1860s, but he was eventually captured and confined to a reservation.

MATTER OF FACT

On many reserves, Native Americans have opened casinos. They use the profits from these casinos to pay for education, housing and health care.

More Blarney

1 Agree or disagree. Support your view with information you have.
- European settlers were kind to reserve land for the use of Native Americans.
- The arrival of horses changed the way of life of the Plains Indians forever.
- In the 19th century, the Choctaw tribe had no knowledge of events outside America.

Tale and Detail

Complete the sentences. Write the answers in your copybook.

	A	B	C	D
The first people to live in North America were	cowboys	Irish emigrants	European settlers	American Indians
Sitting Bull and Crazy Horse were	two Indian tribes	two great Sioux leaders	two powerful spirits	two Europeans
The Sioux defeated General Custer in the	Battle of Trafalgar	Battle of Hastings	Battle of the Little Bighorn	Battle of Clontarf
The ball-game played by Sioux children was called	pemmican	shinny	hurling	squash

Work to Discover

1 When did European settlers first arrive in North America?
2 How did the ability to hunt on horseback affect the Native American culture?
3 What is the Trail of Tears?
4 What effect did the arrival of European settlers have on the health of Native Americans?
5 Describe the ceremonial dress worn by Native Americans to someone who has not seen the drawing on page 49.

Word Wizardry

Character Acrostics

Look at the photograph of Sitting Bull. Complete the character acrostic using the information you have read in this chapter.

Sioux warrior
I
Tribe leader
T
I
N
G

Buffalo hunter
U
L
L

Making Words

Make as many words as you can, using the letters of the word **Cradleboard**.

Surf the Imagination

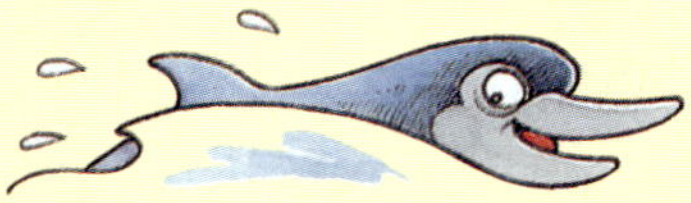

1 Write an account of how you imagine one of the following got his name:
Sitting Bull **Crazy Horse** **Red Cloud** **'The Yawner' (Geronimo)**
2 Make a tepee with poles and canvas or other suitable fabric. Don't forget the smoke flap! Decorate your tepee with paintings of buffalo and other animals OR make a bow and arrow.
3 Devise rules for a new ballgame. Name the game and try it at your next lunchbreak or P.E. lesson.

Mouse Search

1 Native Americans died of common European diseases because they had not developed immunity to them. Find out more about how the human body defends itself from the attack of diseases.
2 Ask your teacher to read extracts about the Trail of Tears from the novel **The Long March** by *Marie-Louise Fitzpatrick* to the class.

Final Answer

What was the original name of the Sioux?

A Florida
B Apache
C Dakota
D Choctaw

Horses

In *The Midnight Fox*, by Betsy Byars, Tom forms an attachment to a black fox on his uncle's farm. People have always depended on animals for food, shelter, work and friendship. In particular, humans have enjoyed a special relationship with horses.

It was Project Time in Fifth Class. After reading about animals in the novel, *The Midnight Fox*, Seán, Anna and Paul had chosen the subject of horses for their project. During Project Time, they discussed what part of the project they would each like to deal with. Their teacher, Ms Dooley, had said they could research information in books, magazines and on the Internet. However, it was very important that they write the project in their own words!

Seán volunteered to write the **introduction**.

Anna decided to write about her own experiences taking care of horses.

Paul chose to write about the evolution of horses through the ages.

The following week at Project Time, they each handed in their work to Ms Dooley.

Introduction by Seán Whelehan

Horses are powerful and graceful animals. For thousands of years, horses have had a special relationship with humans. Early man hunted horses for food. In time, early settlers began to herd them like goats or sheep.

Horses increased in importance to humans when humans discovered that they could '**break them**'. The first record of humans taming horses was in Egypt in 1900 BC. Horses made it possible for people to travel long distances quickly. Carriages, chariots and carts were all pulled by horses, until the train, and later the motor car, replaced them. Horses were also used for work as, because of their great strength, they could pull heavy loads.

Over the years, people learned to breed different types of horses for different purposes. Fast, elegant horses were bred for speed whereas huge, heavy horses were bred for strength. Today there are over 150 different breeds of horse in the world. Although machinery has, for the most part, replaced horses as a means of transport and for lifting heavy loads, the horse is still a hugely popular animal. Horses are now mostly used for recreation and for sports such as racing and showjumping.

The End

My Saturdays with horses by Anna Mainey

I have chosen to write about my experiences with horses. Although I do not own my own horse or pony (I wish I did), my neighbour, Rose, lets me look after her pony, Brandy. I visit Brandy every Saturday. Brandy is a brown **Connemara pony**. She is fully grown and stands thirteen **hands** high. She loves mints!

My first job is to **muck out** Brandy's stable. When I open the half door into the stable, Brandy usually nuzzles into my shoulder to say hello. I lead Brandy outside to the **paddock**. Using a **pitchfork**, I move the clean straw to one side of the stable. When that is done, I fork out the dirty straw into a wheelbarrow. It is heavy work! I wheel the barrow over to the corner of the yard and tip the straw onto the **manure heap**. I go back and sweep the floor of the stable before spreading the clean straw. I usually need to put fresh straw on the floor of the stable. Finally, I check that Brandy's watertrough is full and put more hay in the hay net for her to eat later.

MATTER OF FACT

Horses are measured from the ground to the shoulder in hands. This is a measurement of ten to sixteen centimetres — about the width of a man's knuckles. The age of a horse is measured by examining at its teeth.

When the dirty work is done, I change into my **jodhpurs**, riding jacket, riding boots and riding hat. I have a riding **crop**, but I never use it!

Although, I may be dressed for my riding lesson, Brandy is not! She needs to be **tacked up**. First I brush her down, using a body brush and a **dandy** brush. After every couple of strokes, I have to clean the horsehairs from the brushes using a **curry comb**.

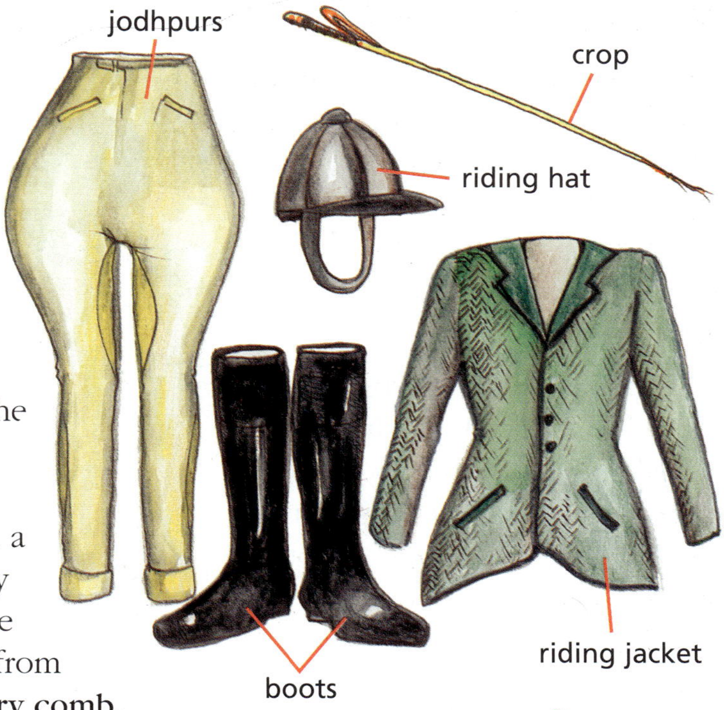

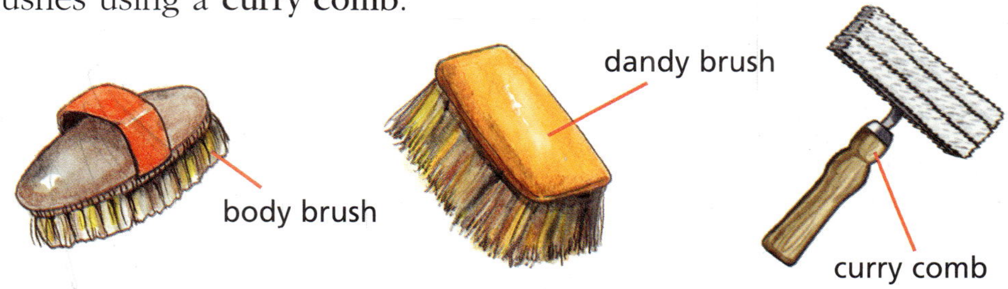

Then I fetch a **bridle**. This is a kind of harness you put on a horse's head. The bridle is attached to reins that you pull on to control the horse's head when you are riding. I place the bridle gently over Brandy's head and ears, making sure she has the **bit** firmly between her teeth. I then drape the reins over her neck.

MATTER OF FACT

A mare is a female horse. Male horses are called **stallions**. **Foals** are baby horses, but after two years foals are called **colts**. Unlike other animals, a foal is born with all its senses. It can see, hear, smell, touch and taste straightaway. It can also walk almost immediately after birth.

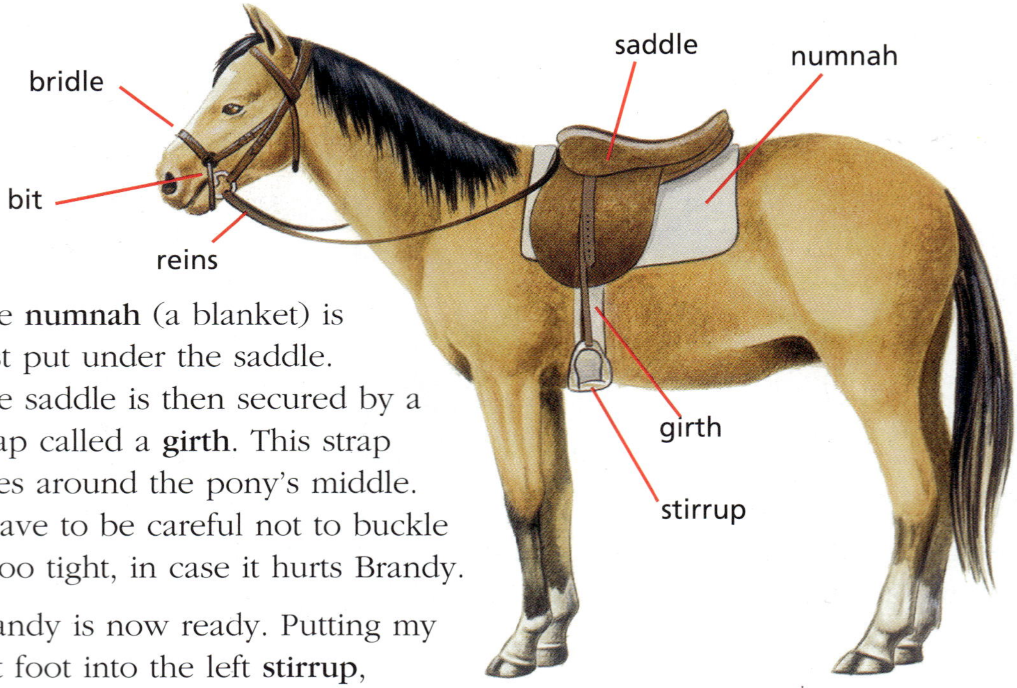

The **numnah** (a blanket) is first put under the saddle. The saddle is then secured by a strap called a **girth**. This strap goes around the pony's middle. I have to be careful not to buckle it too tight, in case it hurts Brandy.

Brandy is now ready. Putting my left foot into the left **stirrup**, I pull myself up. I lower myself gently onto the saddle and off we go. Rose (Brandy's owner) always comes with me on her big mare, Crackers.

When we reach the field, I get Brandy to **trot**.

'Heels down, toes up,' Rose instructs me every time!

She has also taught me how to **canter** and I have recently started jumping. I can only manage the basic jumps. One day, though, I hope to take part in a showjumping competition.

The hour-long lesson is over in no time. When I have put away the saddle and bridle, I give Brandy a quick wipe down with a handful of straw and return her to her stable. Needless to say, I have to give her several mints before I head for home.

Showjumping competition

The history of horses by Paul Sweeney

Horses, zebras and donkeys all belong to the same family of animals. The family can be traced back over sixty million years to an extinct group of mammals.

These mamals were the ancestors of all hoofed animals, including rhinos and tapirs. It is certain they looked nothing like the modern horse.

The first modern relation of the horse was the **Eohippus** or the **Dawn Horse**. It lived in North America about fifty-eight million years ago and it still looked nothing like a horse! It was not much bigger than a rabbit and probably lived in forests. It had small teeth for eating leaves and four toes on its front feet and three toes on its hind feet.

Over the next few million years the Eohippus evolved into the **Mesohippus**. The Mesohippus was larger. It had longer legs and a longer back than the Eohippus. It had three toes on each foot and still looked nothing like a horse!

Horse

Zebra

Donkey

Eohippus

Mesohippus

Over a very long time, the Mesohippus evolved and changed. The great forests of North America, which were its home, disappeared and became grasslands. The Mesohippus had to evolve, to adapt to life on the open plains or die. Their teeth changed to allow them to graze on the grasslands and their necks became longer to assist them to reach down to the ground more easily. Their legs also became longer so they could run faster and thereby escape from predators on the open plains. The central toe became stronger and the other toes began to disappear. The toe nails of the central toes grew down to form the horses, hooves. The Mesohippus had evolved into the **Pliohippus**. The Pliohippus did look something like a horse!

Pliohippus

Equus

Over the last ten million years or so, the Pliohippus evolved into the **Equus**. The Equus looked almost almost identical to the modern horse. So from the Eohippus, to the Mesohippus, to the Pliohippus, at last we have something that looks like a horse! The rest, as they say, is history.

The End

MATTER OF FACT

Equestrian events involve horses. The word *equestrian* comes from the Latin word for horse, *equus*.

MATTER of FACT

The famous fictional horse, Black Beauty, had a star on his forehead. Other horses have different facial markings such as a stripe, white face, blaze, snip and interrupted stripe. The colours of horses have special names. For example **bay horses** are brown horses with black legs, mane and tale.

MATTER of FACT

A horse's eyes are placed on the side of its head, rather than on the front. This allows it to almost see all around it. Horses are now used by police in busy cities.

MATTER of FACT

When a horse is at full gallop, there are times when its four feet do not touch the ground at all!

MATTER of FACT

Many of the world's best showjumping horses are Irish horses. Indeed Ireland has a long and proud tradition for breeding fine **thoroughbred** horses for competition. Perhaps Ireland's most famous horse was **Arkle**, who won the Cheltenham Gold Cup in 1964. His skeleton may be seen in the Irish Horse Museum at the **Irish National Stud** in County Kildare.

More Blarney

Agree or disagree. Support your view with information you have.

- Horses are no longer as important to humans as they once were.
- The evolution of the horse was a long process, taking thousands of years.
- Looking after horses is hard work.
- All horses are the same colour.

Tale and Detail

1 How many breeds of horses are there in the world today?
2 How are horses measured?
3 What is a bridle?
4 What name is given to a saddle-shaped horse blanket?
5 Why do some horses wear blinkers?

Work to Discover

1 Using the information provided on pages 57 and 58, describe in detail the appearance of both horse and rider in the main photograph on page 55.
2 Find two photographs of 'working' horses in this chapter.
3 Describe the appearance of the Eohippus and the Mesohippus to someone who has not seen the illustrations on page 59.
4 Name three sports involving horses depicted in this chapter.
5 Do you find horse-racing exciting to watch? Look at the photograph on page 61 and devise a 'live' commentary for the last thirty seconds of the race. Improvise names for the horses depicted.

Word Wizardry

1 Spelling Rule

Look closely at the following words:

equestrian queen squeal equals require question

What do you notice? In English, **q** is always followed by **u**. Make a class wall-chart of words that follow this rule. Add more as you find them in your reading.

2 Vocabulary: Male, female and young

A male horse is called a stallion. A female horse is called a mare. A young horse is called a foal. Find the male, female and young for each of the following:

sheep fox goat deer pig

3 Use your dictionary to find out what hippopotamus means. Are you surprised?

Surf the Imagination

1. Look back at the illustrations of the Mesohippus and the Pliohippus. Devise your own names for them.
2. Draw or carve a model of a horse
3. Has the horse finally stopped evolving? Draw what you think the horse will look like in a million years.

Mouse Search

1. Choose any animal and trace the stages of its evolution. Illustrate the main stages of the animal's development.
2. Like the horse, humans are also evolving. Study the evolution of man. Draw the main stages in the process.
3. Read **Black Beauty** by *Anna Sewell* and / or **Sunhorse Moonhorse** by *Rosemary Sutcliff*.

Final Answer

The first modern relation of the horse, the Eohippus, is also called:

Agriculture

In *The Selfish Giant*, by Oscar Wilde, the giant had a garden full of plants. He cultivated these plants. Cultivating land for a living is called agriculture. Through history, agriculture has changed the way people live.

Think of all the food you ate in the last two days. Where did all that food come from? Did you buy it in a shop on your way to school? Maybe your parents bought it for you in the supermarket.

How did the shops get the food? They were **supplied** by factories. Every day, vans and trucks deliver food from factories where the food has been **processed** or prepared. So, does food come from factories then? No. Then where do the factories get the food from?

The answer to this question is simple. Food usually comes from farms. Food has to be grown, caught or killed for us to prepare and eat it. Farming has made food so easily available in Ireland, we sometimes take it completely for granted. That would be a mistake.

MATTER OF FACT

The word *agriculture* comes from the Latin word *agricola*, meaning 'farmer'.

Imagine what life would be like if there were no farms! Shops and supermarkets would have very little food to sell. Restaurants would have very little on their menus. Each individual or family group would have to find their own food everyday.

That was what life was like in the Stone Age. In the early Stone Age, food had to be hunted or found. People hunted wild animals or gathered whatever plants and fruits they could find. Hunger was the driving force. There was no time for fun or sport or art. In some seasons, food would be plentiful. On other occasions it would be scarce.

No place had sufficient wildlife or **edible** plants to support a group of people throughout the year. For this reason, people were **nomadic**. They travelled around in family groups and travelled to wherever food could be found. Experts believe the world could not have supported more than four and a half million human beings living in this lifestyle.

emmer

Then, some 10 000 years ago, something happened that would change forever the way people lived. At the end of the last Ice Age, a new type of grass called **emmer** appeared. In time, emmer evolved into the grass now known as **wheat**.

This new grass could be grown in many places around the world, such as the **Fertile Crescent**. The Fertile Crescent is an area we now call the Middle East. Although this area is now dry and **arid**, in 8000 BC the land supported a large number of crops.

People soon recognised that this new grass was a potential source of food. Someone had an idea. Instead of moving from place to place seeking this grass, why not collect the seeds and plant them together in the ground? Better still, why not watch over the plants as they grow and protect them from being eaten by wild animals!

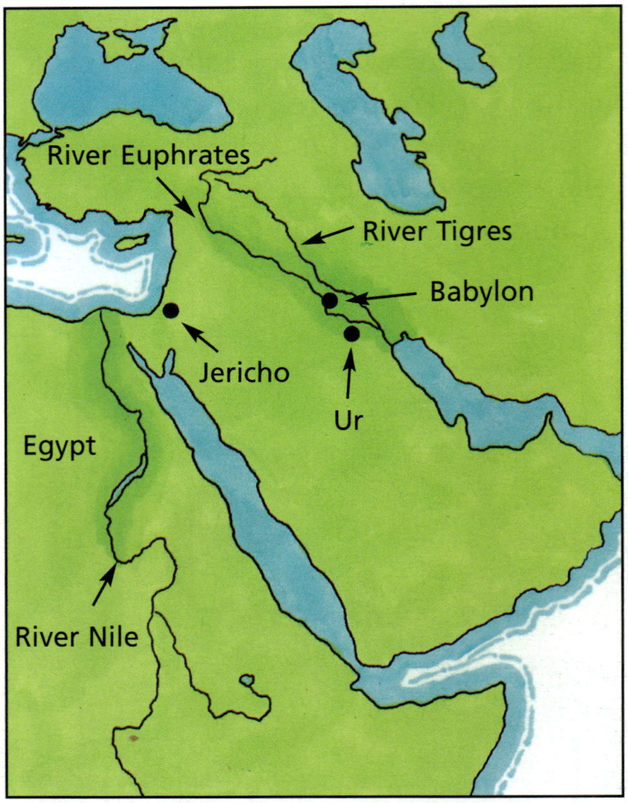

The Fertile Crescent

The first attempts at farming had begun.

People could now remain in one place. A small patch of emmer seeds would provide sufficient food for a family. Family groups began to live together in **settlements**. Each group could help other groups in sowing and harvesting the seeds. They could also protect one another from attacks by wild animals and thieves. Some of these early settlements grew into the first known towns, such as **Jericho** and **Ur** in the Middle East.

Soon people started experimenting with new crops, such as **dates** and **olives**, which up till then had been growing wild. Sheep, goats and other wild animals were tamed and kept for their meat, milk and hide.

For the first time in history, people no longer had to spend all day looking for food. Farmers were there to provide this, which meant that other people could get on with different tasks. Crafts, such as **woodwork**, **toolmaking**, **leatherwork** and **pottery**, developed. As a result life became more **structured** and organised.

MATTER OF FACT

New tools were developed as a result of farming. For example, **sickles** were invented to harvest crops and ploughs were designed to dig the land. Large wild animals such as **oxen** were tamed to assist in this work.

What happens when agriculture fails?

The population of the world has grown enormously over the last 10 000 years and continues to increase. This huge growth would never have happened without the development of farming. There are now more than six billion people in the world today. Will our farmers be able to produce sufficient food in the future? What happens if agriculture fails? The answer is simple — **famine**.

Famine is no stranger to Ireland. In the 19th century, Ireland was struck by a devastating famine. Most of the population depended on one crop as its main source of food. That crop was the potato. In the summer of 1845, the potato plants became infected by a fungus called **blight**. The plants rotted and many people had no food to eat. About one and a half million people died of starvation and illness. A further one million people **emigrated**, many to America. Even when the famine had ended, people continued to emigrate because the country was so poor.

The population of Ireland in 1841 was over eight million. Today the population of the island is less than five million. Had the famine not struck Ireland, our population could have soared to over twenty million, perhaps even higher.

Irish famine scene

Threats to farming

Famine victims

The threat of famine is always present in the world. Every year, in different places around the world, people struggle to grow the food they require. In 1984, Ethiopia suffered a severe **drought**. Across the country, the crops failed in the fields. Thousands of people died of starvation. Fortunately, the rest of the world responded with aid and many lives were saved. Ireland played a major part in helping the people in Ethiopia.

Farming practices around the world sometimes have a harmful effect on the environment. In Ireland, overuse of **fertilisers** and **animal slurry** has caused river pollution. Over-grazing by cattle, sheep and goats has left grassland like desert. Vital forests have been cleared and this has led to precious soil being **exposed** and washed or blown away. Land has been **overfarmed** and is now incapable of supporting a crop.

In recent times, aid organisations have been established to help farmers to find better ways to use their land. **Bóthar** is an Irish aid agency which provides farm animals and farming advice to Third World communities.

Solutions

Irish aid agencies such as **Trocaire**, **Concern** and **GOAL** work tirelessly to help those in danger of starvation. These agencies need our help. There is plenty of food in the world — the problem is that the food does not necessarily grow where it is most needed. International aid agencies frequently comment on the need for a **fairer distribution** of food resources.

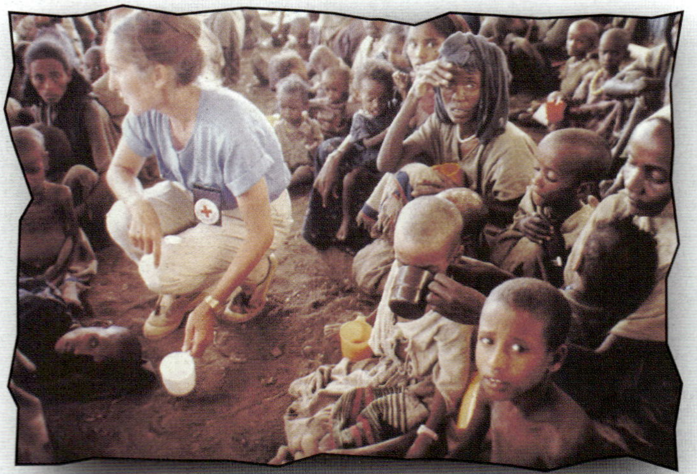

Red Cross worker in an African village

There is an old saying 'give a man a fish and you will feed him for a day — give him a fishing rod and he will be able to feed himself for the rest of his life'.

In recent years, **agriculturalists** and **scientists** have worked together to find new ways of producing the food we need, without harming the environment. Farming, one of our earliest crafts, is now supported by technology to face the challenges of feeding a growing world population safely.

MATTER OF FACT

Traditionally, farm produce has been Ireland's biggest export, earning a lot of money for the country. The Irish food industry is one of our biggest employers.

MATTER OF FACT

The energy content of food is measured in **calories**. Adults require 2 000 to 2 500 calories per day. The average daily consumption in Ireland is 3 952 calories per day. The lowest average daily consumption in the world is in Somalia in Africa. It is just 1 499 calories per day. Remember — food is not distributed fairly around the world.

MATTER OF FACT

Bob Geldof is an Irish musician, committed to helping famine victims throughout the world. In 1984, he launched a **famine relief programme** called **Band Aid** to help the starving people in Ethiopia. He organised thirty-six pop stars to record a song called *Do they know it's Christmas?* The record became the best-selling single of the year and raised over £5 million sterling for Ethiopia. Geldof organised a major concert in London and Philadelphia (USA) called **Live Aid**. This concert, held on 13 July 1985, raised £70 million sterling for Ethiopia. In recognition of his work, Bob Geldof was **knighted** and nominated for a Nobel Prize.

More Blarney

Agree or disagree. Support your view with information you have.

- In the early Stone Age, people had plenty of leisure time.
- People were nomadic because they got bored living in one place.
- The discovery of emmer changed the course of history.
- Farming harms the environment.

Tale and Detail

Complete the sentences. Write the answers in your copybook.

	A	B	C	D
Emmer evolved into	rice	potato	wheat	chicken
The Fertile Crescent is in	Offaly	Italy	USA	The Middle East
A sickle is	a farming implement	a disease	an animal	a type of crop
'Band Aid' was organised by	Bono	Robbie Williams	Bob Geldof	Britney Spears
The World's population is	about 6 million	about 6 billion	about 60 billion	about 600 000

Work to Discover

Complete the following sentences:

1. The Famine in Ireland was caused by…
2. Trócaire, Concern and GOAL…
3. 'Band Aid' recorded the song…
4. Calories measure…

Word Wizardry

Sayings and proverbs

'Give a man a fish and you will feed him for a day – give him a fishing rod and he will be able to feed himself for the rest of his life.'

What does this saying mean? Discuss with your partner or group the meaning of the following sayings:

'Laugh and the whole world laughs with you, cry and you cry alone.'

'The darkest hour is that before the dawn.'

'There is no argument equal to a happy smile.'

Proverbs: The names of the Irish Aid Agencies Trócaire and Gorta are Irish words. Use your dictionary / foclóir to find the meaning of these words.

Surf the Imagination

1. Look at a menu for a restaurant or take-away. Pick out the words used to make the dishes sound as appetising as possible. Now devise your menu for a three-course meal. Describe each dish and decorate your menu.
2. Listen to the song *Do they know it's Christmas?* Do you recognise any of the voices?
3. Write the lyrics (words) for your own song about famine relief. Then set it to music!

Mouse Search

1. Look up a recipe for making bread. What ingredients are needed? With permission, try to make your own bread, either at school or at home, by following the recipe.
2. Find out what conditions are necessary for seeds to germinate. Grow some cress and mustard seeds on tissue paper in the classroom.
3. Check the packaging on all the packaged food you eat this week (e.g. bar of chocolate, cereal box, packet of sweets). Look at the list of ingredients. Check the nutritional content of each. Are you surprised by anything you discovered?

Final Answer

Famine is caused by:

A a shortage of food in the world
B unfair distribution of the world's resources
C a growing world population
D fertilisers and animal slurry

Friends and enemies

In the novel *The Good Liar*, by Gregory Maguire, Marcel is helped by an enemy soldier. Warfare has always been a part of our history. Is war ever worth the suffering it causes?

It was a mess. Soon after we launched the attack, I was cut off from my unit. The buildings and streets were nothing but rubble. Machine-gun fire burst and crackled nearby. Plaster exploded a few metres away from me as wild gunfire whizzed through the air. I needed to find cover quickly.

The floor of the building collapsed almost as soon as I ran into it. I found myself falling into darkness. The dust settled and my leg and shoulder began to ache. My eyes gradually grew accustomed to the gloom.

Then I saw him. He was about the same age as me. Like me, he was injured. His uniform and helmet were different to mine. He was the enemy and here we were, both trapped in a ruined basement. Neither of us would get out of here on our own. Was it time for us to lay our weapons aside and consider a **truce**?

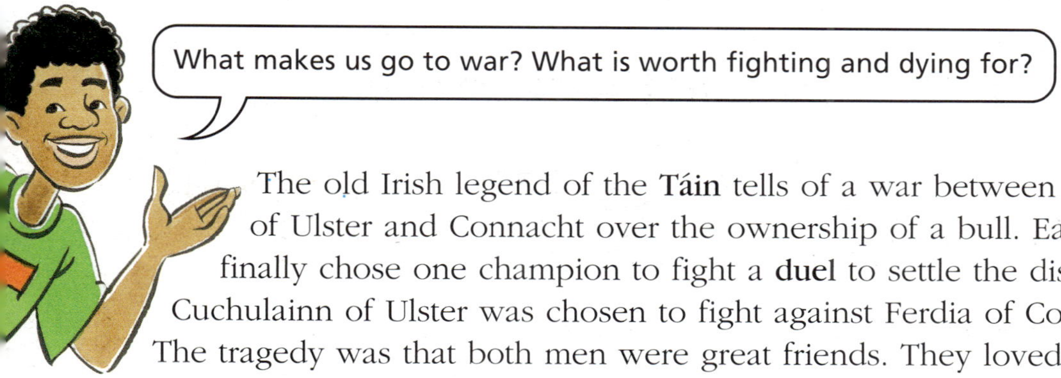

The old Irish legend of the **Táin** tells of a war between the people of Ulster and Connacht over the ownership of a bull. Each side finally chose one champion to fight a **duel** to settle the dispute. Cuchulainn of Ulster was chosen to fight against Ferdia of Connacht. The tragedy was that both men were great friends. They loved one another like brothers. Neither man wanted to fight the other. In the end, Cuchulainn killed Ferdia and Ulster won the war.

The Táin is only a legend, but in real life, friends, neighbours and even families have been bitterly divided by **civil war**. A civil war is a war between people from the same country.

In 1861, a dispute arose in the United States of America. Eleven states in the south of the country decided to split from the states in the north. The southern states depended on the labour of slaves. By this time, however, slavery had been abolished in the north. The new president, Abraham Lincoln, decided to abolish slavery all over the country. More than half a million people died in the civil war that followed.

American Civil War

Abraham Lincoln

Many Irishmen who had **emigrated** to the USA found themselves fighting on different sides in the American Civil War.

Soldiers at a checkpoint during the War of Independence

Sixty years later, a civil war broke out in Ireland. Ireland had been fighting a War of Independence with Britain between 1919 and 1921. In 1921, the British and Irish signed a **peace treaty**. This treaty allowed Ireland to rule twenty-six out of the thirty-two counties of Ireland. Six of the counties in Ulster were to remain part of Britain.

The Irish **Free State** was born — but it was a divided state. Some saw this arrangement as a huge step forward towards gaining full independence. Others bitterly opposed it. Men and women who had fought side by side for independence were now sworn enemies. The newborn state of Ireland was torn apart by a bitter civil war. The conflict lasted from 1921 until 1923.

In the end, as in all conflicts, the two sides had to sit down around the table and settle their differences. Words took the place of bullets.

Bombs left many buildings in Ireland completely destroyed

In the 20th century, two major wars were fought, involving many countries around the world. These wars changed the world forever and resulted in terrible **casualties**. The wars have since been called World War I and World War II.

World War I (1914 – 1918)

In August 1914, Europe was plunged into war. Germany and the **central powers** (Austria, Hungary, Bulgaria and Turkey) were at war with Britain, France, Russia and their **allies** (Belgium, Cyprus, Greece, Italy, Japan, Portugal, Romania, Serbia and the USA). They were fighting over control of land.

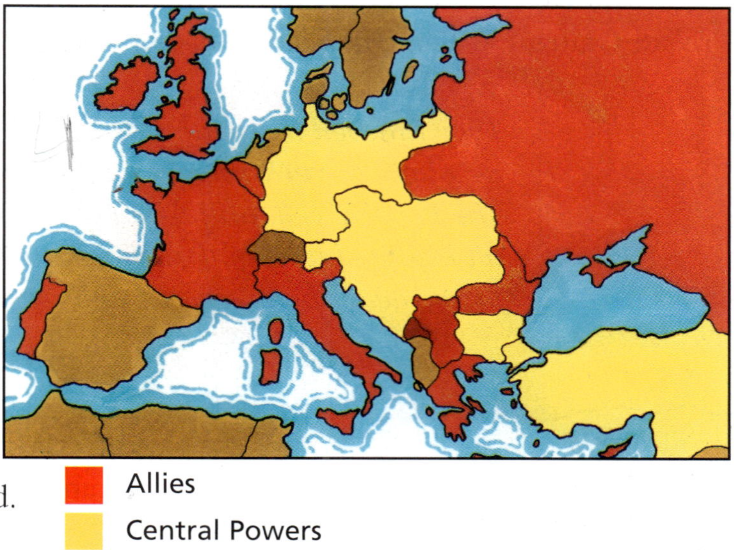

Young men on both sides were encouraged to join the army and fight for their country. Thousands of young Irishmen **enlisted** to fight on the side of Britain. They were told … 'It'll be over by Christmas'.

But it was not over by Christmas. Instead, hundreds of thousands of soldiers ended up in filthy **trenches**, surrounded by barbed wire, mud and the bodies of fallen comrades and enemies. Thousands of men died in battles to gain a few metres of land. The next day, the same few metres could be lost in another equally costly battle.

MATTER of FACT

About ten million people were killed in World War I and about twice that number were injured or **maimed**.

French soldiers during World War I

However, on Christmas Day 1914, something happened in the trenches in eastern France. The soldiers on both sides declared an unofficial truce. Strange lights began to appear along the German trenches. British and French soldiers quickly realised that these were candles lighting on small trees. Then came the sound of a hymn ... *Silent Night*, sung in German.

Private Graham Williams, a British soldier, recalled ...

> *They finished their carol and we thought that we ought to* ***retaliate*** *in some way, so we sang The First Nowell, and when we finished, they all began clapping; they then struck up another favourite of theirs ... and so it went on.*
>
> *From 1914 – 1918 by Winter and Baggett, BBC*

Soldiers in the trenches

Not a shot was fired. Greetings were shouted across **No Man's Land**. Men from both sides climbed out of the trenches to recover the bodies of friends who had been killed days or even weeks earlier. Soldiers who had tried to kill one another stood about in the mud and chatted. They even organised a few games of football. Some began to hope that the truce would continue.

However, commanding officers were appalled and gave strict orders for any show of friendship to end. Within days, the killing began again. The war dragged on until the eleventh hour of the eleventh day of the eleventh month of 1918 when the Germans finally surrendered.

World War II (1939 – 1945)

Modern technology gave warring nations the ability to inflict even more damage on one another. Between 1939 and 1945, many countries all over the world were engaged in a second world war. World War II saw entire cities **levelled** by bombing raids. The British city of Coventry and the German city of Dresden were both completely destroyed.

Towards the end of the war, the Americans inflicted heavy casualties on the Japanese. In March 1945, Japan's capital city, Tokyo, suffered a major **air raid**. More than 83 000 people were killed and 41 000 were injured.

World War II came to an end when **atomic bombs** were dropped on the Japanese cities of Hiroshima and Nagasaki. Over 100 000 people were killed instantly when the bomb fell on Hiroshima. A further 55 000 died of their injuries within a year.

Caen in northern France following bombing raids

MATTER OF FACT

An estimated fifty-eight million lives were lost during World War II. Russia (or the **USSR**, as it was then known) paid the highest price. About twenty million Russians died. Over one million people, Russians and Germans, died in one battle alone — the Battle of Stalingrad.

The Road to Peace

The League of Nations

The horrific loss of life in World War I prompted many countries to try to find a way of avoiding conflict. In 1919, the **League of Nations** was founded by forty countries to prevent future wars. However, it did not prevent World War II from breaking out in 1939. It would take the greater loss of life from this war to bring about the founding of the **United Nations** (UN).

The UN was founded in 1945. Like the League of Nations, the UN also aims at maintaining peace all over the world. The UN has tried to act as a 'referee' between countries that are hostile to one another.

Ireland plays a very active role in the work of the UN. Irish troops have served as peacekeepers in places such as Cyprus, the Congo, Lebanon, the former Yugoslavia and East Timor.

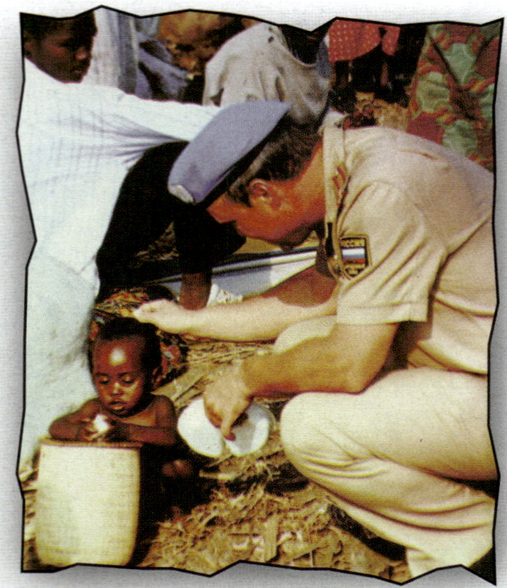

UN peacekeepers at work

UN headquarters, New York

There is a saying *The dove builds its nest slowly*. This means that it takes time and effort to make peace. The dove is a symbol of peace. For many people in warn-torn regions, peace is a very precious and rare thing.

MATTER OF FACT

On average, for every soldier who has been killed in battle, about nine civilians have also died.

MATTER OF FACT

The longest continuous war in history was the **Thirty Years War**. It was fought between various European countries from 1618 to 1648. History books mention the **Hundred Years War** between France and England during the Middle Ages. This was actually a collection of smaller wars, rather than one continuous bout of fighting.

MATTER OF FACT

The shortest war took place on 27 August 1896 between Britain and the African state of Zanzibar. It started at nine o'clock in the morning and was over forty-five minutes later.

MATTER OF FACT

The atomic bomb was a symbol of a new age in warfare — the **nuclear age**. From the 1950s until the breakup of the Soviet Union in 1991, a **Cold War** existed between America and the USSR. A Cold War means a war without fighting — only political hostility. During the Cold War, both sides began building thousands of nuclear weapons aimed at each other. Had either side attacked, the other would have responded. Every nation on earth would have been wiped out.

More Blarney

1 Agree or disagree. Support your view with information you have.
   - War is never worth the suffering it causes.
   - War does not affect civilians.
   - Technology has meant an increase in the amount of arms in the world.
   - Killing in war is not murder.

2 What do you think the events of Christmas Day 1914 tell us about soldiers?

Tale and Detail

Complete the sentences. Write the answers in your copybook.

	A	B	C	D
Who abolished slavery in the USA?	Bill Clinton	Bertie Ahern	Abraham Lincoln	George W Bush
How many counties were there in the Irish Free State?	thirty-two	twenty-six	twenty-three	six
What are the dates of World War I?	1939 - 1945	1914 - 1918	1919 - 1921	1814 - 1818
On what cities did atomic bombs fall?	Coventry and Dresden	Hiroshima and Nagasaki	London and Manchester	Jericho and Ur

Work to Discover

1 What is a civil war?
2 How did the British retaliate to the German soldiers singing on Christmas Day 1914?
3 Where is 'No Man's Land'?
4 In World War I, on what date did Germany surrender?
5 Why was the League of Nations founded? Did it achieve its aim?
6 What could have happened if either America or the USSR had attacked during the Cold War?

Word Wizardry

UN stands for United Nations. **USA** stands for United States of America. What do the following stand for?

GAA	**AIB**	**EU**	**BBC**	**ISPCA**	**FBI**
RTE	**FAI**	**CIE**	**NATO**	**ESB**	**WHO**

Sayings and Proverbs:

'The dove builds its nest slowly' is a saying or proverb. Make a class collection of proverbs by choosing one, writing it out and decorating it.

Surf the Imagination

Imagine you are one of the soldiers involved in the Christmas Day truce of 1914. Write a letter to a family member, telling him / her of this experience.

The dove is a symbol for peace. Design a poster to promote world peace using your own symbol for peace.

Mouse Search

1 Read the story of the Táin Bó Cuailgne. (The Brown Bull of Cooley)

2 Look at a map of Ireland. List the twenty-six counties of the Irish Free State. List the counties that became part of the United Kingdom.

3 If you like stories about children during wartime, read the following:
The Good Liar by *Gregory Maguire*
Safe Harbour by *Marita Conlon McKenna*
Carrie's War by *Nina Bawden*
The Diary of Anne Frank by *Anne Frank*

Final Answer

How many lives are estimated to have been lost in World War II?

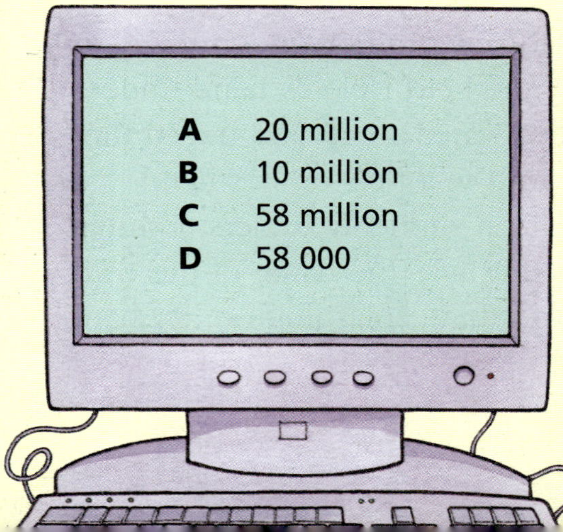

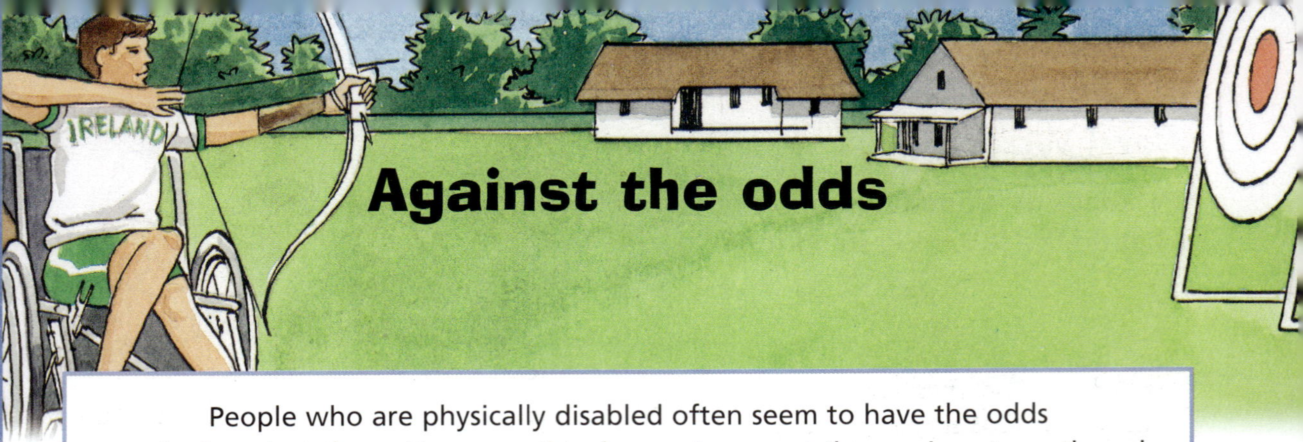

Against the odds

People who are physically disabled often seem to have the odds stacked against them. However, this does not prevent them using strength and determination to achieve worldwide success.

Helen Keller

Helen Keller's story gives courage and hope to anyone coping with difficulties in life. Helen was born in America in 1880. She was a perfectly happy little girl until, when she was nineteen months old, she became seriously ill and almost died. She was left deaf and blind. She could not learn how to talk because she could not hear. Her world was dark and silent. Her life was a nightmare.

Then her parents found her a teacher called Anne Sullivan. Anne used Helen's sense of touch to communicate with her. Patiently she would 'spell' out the name of whatever Helen touched on to the palm of her hand. The problem was that Helen did not understand that c-a-t meant cat or that d-o-l-l meant doll!

However, one wonderful day, Anne held Helen's hand under the water pump and traced the word w-a-t-e-r on her hand. Helen suddenly understood that *water* was the name of the cold, wet thing splashing on her hand!

A young Helen Keller with her teacher Anne Sullivan

Helen Keller with Anne Sullivan

A door had opened in Helen's life. Everyday she learned new words. By tracing the words onto someone's hand, she could 'talk' to them. She was very curious and she learned quickly.

Next Helen learned how to read and write **Braille**. Braille is a special system of writing for the blind. The letters are made up of raised dots on the paper which blind people touch to read. Helen also learned how to speak. She practised this by touching her teacher's lips or tongue and copying the movement. It was difficult, but she **persevered** and in the end she succeeded.

Anne accompanied Helen when she went to school and later to University. As the teachers spoke, Anne 'spelt' the lessons on to Helen's hands and helped her with her homework in the evenings. Later, Helen devoted her life to helping people with special needs. She travelled the world, gave speeches and wrote extensively. At the age of twenty-two years, she wrote her **autobiography**, *The Story of my Life*. She died in 1968 at the age of eighty years.

Helen Keller in later life

MATTER OF FACT

Braille was invented by Louis Braille in 1829. He himself was blind from the age of three years.

Heather Mills

Heather Mills is a fashion model — with a difference!

Heather had a difficult childhood. Her mother abandoned her when she was nine years. Her father eventually ended up in jail. When she was thirteen years old, Heather ran away, sleeping rough in London's Waterloo Station like many homeless children. However, she was determined to succeed in life and she dreamed of becoming a model.

A friend of Heather's secretly sent her photograph to the *Daily Mirror* newspaper's 'Dreamgirl Competition'. Heather won. Her modelling career had begun.

In 1990, war broke out in Yugoslavia where Heather was working as a model. She used the money she earned from modelling to help disabled victims of the war.

It was on her return to England, in August 1993, that Heather was involved in a terrible accident. A police motorcycle ran into her, as she was crossing the road. Her left leg had to be **amputated** just below the knee. However, whereas most people would have been devastated by this, Heather turned this disaster into success.

Heather Mills

Heather was fitted with an artificial limb. The nature of her injury meant that this artificial leg had to be frequently replaced. Heather realised that she could put the discarded artificial legs to good use, by sending them to victims of landmine explosions in Yugoslavia.

Heather Mills with Paul McCartney

Not content with that, Heather appealed to others in her position to donate their 'old limbs'. By 2001, her organisation had given over 27 000 limbs to landmine victims!

Heather's autobiography, *Out on a Limb*, is a bestseller. All the money raised from the sales of the book was donated to charity. In 1996, she was nominated for a Nobel Prize and in 1999 she received a 'People of the Year' award. Indeed, there is now an award named after her — 'The Heather Mills Award'.

Heather still models successfully and runs half marathons for charity. As she says, 'any time I was challenged and told I couldn't do something, I would absolutely have to prove the opposite and I did.' Her achievements in the face of so many obstacles gives courage to anyone facing challenges in their own lives.

Andrea Bocelli

Another person who refused to allow a handicap to stand in his way is the singer, Andrea Bocelli. Andrea was **visually impaired** from the day he was born and when he was twelve years old, a football accident left him totally blind. However, blindness was never allowed to get in the way of Andrea Bocelli's ambitions. His parents recognised his musical talent when he was still very young and he began learning the piano at age six. Later he learnt to play the flute and the saxophone.

His singing career really started in 1993 when he accompanied the singer Zucchero on a European tour. The beauty and depth of Andrea's voice soon earned him many followers. He frequently received standing ovations for his performances. In 1994, the most famous opera singer in the world, Luciano Pavarotti, invited Andrea to sing with him. On Christmas Eve of that year, Andrea performed for the Pope.

In 1995, Andrea's song, *Con te Partiro*, was top of the charts in France for six weeks. In Belgium, the song broke the record by remaining at the top of the charts for twelve weeks. One of his **duets** with the soprano, Sarah Brightman, *Time to say Goodbye*, has sold almost three million copies and has made Andrea Bocelli famous throughout the world.

Christopher Nolan

Christopher Nolan is a very successful Irish writer. Writing is hugely important to Christopher — it is his only means of communication.

Christopher suffered **brain damage** when he was born. As a result of this, his body was completely paralysed. For years, he lived in the silent prison of his body, unable to talk to his family or friends.

However, when Christopher was eleven years old, a teacher, Eva Fitzpatrick, noticed that he had some control over the movement of his head.
She attached a 'pointer' to Christopher's forehead. By tapping this pointer on typewriter keys, Christopher was able to write. This is how he describes his first-time typing:

> Together they would struggle, the boy blowing like a whale from the huge effort of trying to discipline his bedamned body. Every tip of his pointer to the keys of the typewriter sent his body sprawling backwards. Eva held his chin in her hands and waited for him to relax and tip another key… But for Eva Fitzpatrick, he would never have broken free.

From *Under the Eye of the Clock* by Christopher Nolan.

Christopher did not stop there. In 1981, at the age of fifteen, a collection of his poems called *Dam-burst of Dreams* was published. He won the **Whitbread Literary Award** for his autobiography, *Under the Eye of the Clock*, in 1987. His most recent book is called *The Banyan Tree*.

The young Christopher Nolan

The Paralympic Games

The **Paralympic Games** are the second largest sporting event in the world, after the Olympic Games. They provide disabled athletes with the opportunity to compete in sporting events.

The first Paralympic Games were held in 1948, when a small group of disabled war **veterans** held a sports meeting at the Stoke Mandeville Hospital in England. The Games **coincided** with the Olympic Games, which were being held in London. The Paralympics were held again in Rome in 1960 — immediately following the Rome Olympic Games. The Paralympic Games are now held after every Olympic Games.

Catherina McKiernan with members of the Irish Squad for the Sydney Paralympics 2000

Ireland's Tim Culhane, who took part in the Judo competition at the Paralympics

Irish athletes with disabilities have competed successfully in the Paralympic Games since the Games in Rome in 1960. Ireland sent a squad of thirty-nine athletes to the Sydney Paralympics in the year 2000. The team won nine medals — five gold, three silver and one bronze.

MATTER OF FACT

Paralympic means *parallel*, (not **paraplegic**, as is often thought), because they run 'parallel' to the Olympic Games.

MATTER OF FACT

Heather Mills is not the only model with artificial legs. Aimee Mullins had her legs amputated at the knees when she was twelve months old.
Like Heather Mills, she wears artificial legs.
Aimee is also an athlete and has broken sprinting records for **double amputees**. Her 'running legs' are based on the legs of a cheetah, the fastest living animal on earth.

MATTER OF FACT

Christy Browne, who died in 1981, was another Irish writer who was also disabled. He had to learn to write with his left foot. His humourous autobiography, *My Left Foot*, was made into an Oscar-winning film.

MATTER OF FACT

Stephen Hawking is the most famous living scientist in the world today. He is Professor of Mathematics at Cambridge University in England, but his most important work has been in the area of astronomy. His book, *A Brief History of Time*, was on the bestseller list in England for a record period in excess of four years.
Stephen Hawking's achievements are more remarkable because, since the 1960s, he has suffered from a **neurological** (brain) disease called **Lou Gehrig's Disease**. As a result, he is confined to a wheelchair and is unable to move his body. He can only speak with the aid of a computer.

More Blarney

G 1 Agree or disagree. Support your view with information you have.
- Everybody is talented in some way.
- The people we read about in this chapter have nothing in common.
- Stories like these inspire us when faced with challenges in life.
- The teachers of Helen Keller and Christopher Nolan were of no use to them.

P 2 Share, with your partner, what you think is your greatest achievement to date. Say why you are proud of it.

Tale and Detail

Complete the sentences. Write the answers in your copybook.

	A	B	C	D
Special writing for the blind is called	shorthand	Braille	typing	print
Heather Mills encouraged others	to throw away old limbs	to donate old limbs to landmine victims	to become models	to write their autobiographies
Andrea Bocelli's special talent is	painting	singing	acting	playing football
At the Sydney Paralympics, the Irish team won	no medals	nine medals	five medals	three medals

Work to Discover

Who is it? Identify the person from the hint below.

1 She was Helen Keller's teacher.
2 *Out on a Limb* is her autobiography.
3 He is the most famous living scientist.
4 She was Christopher Nolan's teacher.
5 Her 'running legs' are based on the legs of a cheetah.
6 He invented special writing, which enables the blind to read.
7 His autobiography is called *Under the Eye of the Clock*.

Word Wizardry

Adjectives

Think of any adjectives that describe the people you have read about. Say which of the following apply and why.

lazy	determined	brave	selfish	defeated
eager	persevering	stubborn	hardworking	self-pitying
bitter	angry	inspiring	positive	ambitious

Surf the Imagination

1. Close your eyes for one minute. Listen to the sounds inside and outside the classroom. Jot down all the sounds you heard. Write a poem entitled 'Sounds'.
2. Imagine you have an opportunity to interview one of the people that you read about in this chapter. Make a list of questions you would like to ask him or her.
3. Make a plan for your autobiography. Choose a title. Write the chapter headings to signal the most important events in your life so far. Write the opening paragraph of your autobiography.

Mouse Search

Our Five Senses

1. What are the five senses? Which of the five senses do you think is the most important? Why do you say so?
2. Write a word in **Braille** by punching holes in a page. Ask your partner to try to decipher the word.
3. Ask your teacher to read **My Ship** by Christy Browne to the class.

Final Answer

My Left Foot is the autobiography of

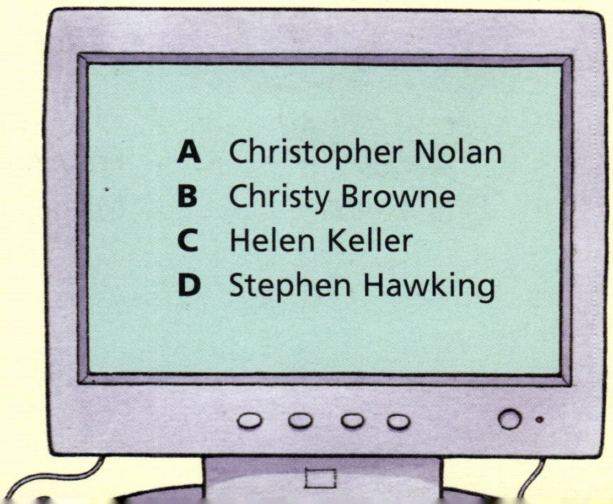

A trip to the National Gallery

Everyone is welcome to visit the National Gallery of Ireland. It is located in Merrion Square in Dublin city. There is plenty to see! The Gallery has a fine collection of paintings, drawings and sculptures from all over the world. These are just a few examples of the works of art in the collection.

The painting on next page is called *The Taking of Christ*. It is by **Caravaggio**.

1 What do you think is happening in the painting? Does the title give you any clues?

2 Describe the people in the painting.

3 Who do you think is the most important person in the painting? Why do you think this?

4 Some areas of the painting are very dark and others are very bright. Where do you think the light is coming from?

5 What do you notice about the clothes the people are wearing? Do they seem heavy and 'real'? How does the artist **convey** this?

Mouse Search

1 Find out more about the following Italian artists: Fra Angelico, Giotto, Donatello, Leonardo da Vinci, Michelangelo and Raphael.

Michelangelo Merisi da Caravaggio (1573-1610) came from the village of Caravaggio in Northern Italy. He was an intense and dramatic person and these **traits** are visible in his paintings. His figures often show great emotion and their expressions and gestures are full of energy. Caravaggio painted people exactly as he saw them, unlike other painters of the time.

J B Yeats
1900

This painting is a **portrait** of the poet William Butler Yeats. It was painted by his father, John Butler Yeats.

1 Describe the sitter in this painting.
How many articles of his clothing can you make out?

2 Is the sitter happy or sad? How can you tell?

3 Can you tell anything about the personality of the sitter from this painting?

4 Is this a colourful painting? Why do you think the painter chose to use these colours in the painting?

5 Do you think the sitter looks solid and three-dimensional? How do you think the artist created this effect?

6 What is unusual about where the artist signed the painting? Why do you think he did this?

John Butler Yeats (1839-1922) was a portrait painter. Although he trained as a barrister, he preferred to work as an artist. In 1908, he emigrated to New York, where he remained for the remainder of his life. He was the father of a very gifted family. His son, William, became Ireland's most famous poet, winning the Nobel Prize for Literature in 1923. His other son, Jack, is one of Ireland's most celebrated painters. Many of Jack's works, including *The Liffey Swim*, *Grief* and *The Singing Horseman* may be seen in the National Gallery of Ireland. His daughters, Elizabeth and Susan (nicknamed 'Lollie' and 'Lily'), played important roles in developing arts and crafts in Ireland. Their portraits may also be seen in the National Gallery of Ireland.

Mouse Search

1 Find out what you can about a member of the Yeats family. You may choose between:

William Butler Yeats
Jack Butler Yeats
Elizabeth Butler Yeats
Susan Butler Yeats

The painting on page 101 is called *La Ferme de Lezaven*, Finistere. It is by Roderic O'Conor. It is a **landscape**.

1 Is this painting realistic?

2 Is there much detail in the painting?
Are the shapes of trees, flowers and buildings very distinct?

3 Did the painter used a lot of paint?
Do you see the marks of the brush on the **canvas**?

4 What strikes you most about the colours in this painting?

5 Do you think it was a hot or a cold day? Why?

MATTER OF FACT

Impressionism is the name given to an artistic movement which began in France in the 19th century. Impressionist painters mostly painted outdoors and their paintings are full of light and colour. They were not concerned with reproducing details of what they saw. They wanted to give their audience an 'impression' of what they were painting.
In *La Ferme de Lezaven*, Finistere, Roderic O'Conor gives the 'impression' of trees, flowers, heat and light using **vibrant**, contrasting colours and small, thin brush-strokes.

This painting by the French Impressionist painter, Monet, is called *A River Scene, Autumn*. When critics first saw Monet's work in 1874, they thought it was ridiculous. They used the term 'Impressionists' to describe the artists who painted in this style.
The term was meant to be insulting, but it was soon used to describe the entire movement.

Roderic O'Conor (1860-1940) was an Impressionist painter. He was born in County Roscommon, the son of wealthy parents and he never had to worry about money. He had the opportunity to study painting in England, Spain and France. He was greatly influenced by the work of the Impressionists. He is considered to be Ireland's best-known artist internationally. His work is very similar to that of the famous Dutch painter, Van Gogh.

This painting is by Mainie Jellett.
It is called *Achill Horses*.

1 How many horses do you see in this painting?

2 Is the painting realistic or imaginary?

3 Are the horses painted in detail?

4 What other shapes do you see in the painting?

5 How many colours can you see?

6 Do you find the title of the picture puzzling? Have you any idea why she called it *Achill Horses* when there does not seem to be anything about Achill in the picture?

MATTER OF FACT

Mainie Jellett was a **Cubist** painter. **Cubism** was an art movement that began in Paris in 1907. Until then, painters attempted to represent three-dimensional objects using painting techniques such as **shading**. Cubist painters, however, wanted to portray images in a different way. Cubists tried to show the object from all angles. They did this by breaking up the object, or flattening it and painting it in an **abstract** way.

Work to Discover

1 Write five questions about this chapter.
2 List three facts that you remember from this chapter.

Surf the Imagination

1 Imagine you are a great artist. What **medium** (paint, sculpture, drawing, photography) would you use? Describe the works of art you would create.
2 Draw, paint or make a model of someone you know.
3 Research the work of the Cubist painters Pablo Picasso and Georges Braque.

Mary Harriet (Mainie) Jellett (1897-1944) was born in Dublin. She was an accomplished pianist, as well as a painter. Her early teachers were the Yeats sisters, Lily and Lollie. She studied in Dublin and London and later in Paris, where she became interested in Cubism. She first exhibited her work in Dublin in 1920. Later she taught and promoted cubism and other modern art styles in Ireland.

Drugs

In the novel, *A Woman of Aran*, Bridget Gillan Dirrane describes herbal cures that were used to treat illnesses on the Aran Islands. All drugs need to be handled carefully. Drugs save lives, but they can cause misery and destruction, if they are abused.

Plants have many chemicals in their leaves, stems and roots. These chemicals help the plants to grow, they protect them from disease and even defend them from attack.

Throughout the ages, people have discovered many uses for chemicals produced by plants. Many of these chemicals cure illness. Every year, large **pharmaceutical** (drug) companies spend millions of euros studying plants all over the world in search of new drugs.

Here are a few examples of the **herbal remedies** some plants provide:

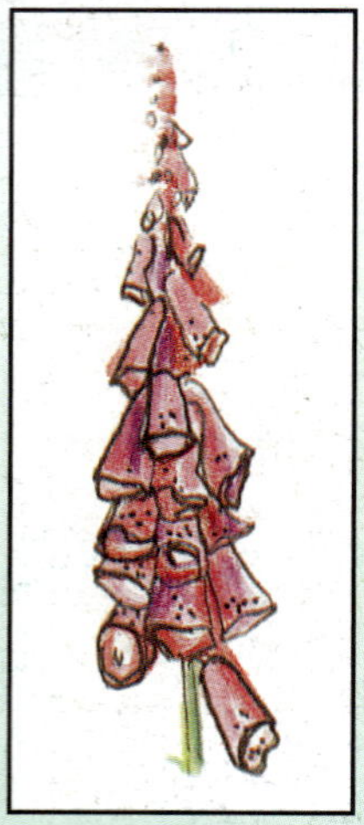

Foxglove

Produces **digitalis** (used to treat heart conditions)

Dock leaves

Contain **anti-histamines** (good for allergies)

Blackcurrants

Contain aspirin (a painkiller)

Cloves

Contain an **antiseptic** and also relieve toothache

Cumin

Is used to treat asthma

In earlier times, knowledge of herbal remedies was passed from generation to generation. Herbal cures were frequently the only medicine available. The Ancient Greeks used **sap** from the bark of the willow tree as a painkiller. Willow bark contains aspirin.

Ergot is a type of fungus that affects cereals such as barley. Eating a food infected by ergot can cause a personality change. This is because a chemical in ergot affects the way a person's brain works and causes strange behaviour. Experts now believe that stories of people who were 'bewitched' or 'possessed by demons' may well have suffered ergot poisoning.

The effects of ergot poisoning

MATTER OF FACT

Your garden may have of plants that could kill or cure you! For instance, every part of the deadly **monkshood** plant is poisonous. On the other hand, the **vinca** or **periwinkle** plant contains a chemical used to treat cancer.

monkshood

Grass infected with ergot disease

The opium poppy grows naturally across Southern Asia. Sap from this plant is used to make opium. For years, opium was used as a painkiller. Like ergot, it contains chemicals that change the normal function of the brain. Doctors use opium to temporarily 'turn off' pain suffered by seriously injured people.

Unfortunately, others use opium for pleasure. Opium interferes with the brain's normal function and can cause a person to see, hear, think and feel differently. People quickly become **addicted** to this sensation. Afterwards, they feel a desperate need for more of the drug. This is called an **addiction**. Opium addicts require the drug again and again and end up spending their lives in a confused, hazy trance.

An opium poppy

Opium may be **refined** (made purer) into stronger drugs called **opiates**. One such drug is **morphine**. During the American Civil War, doctors used morphine to treat seriously injured soldiers. After the war, many of these men still had a craving for the drug. They were addicted. Morphine is used today as a powerful painkiller. It is administered very carefully.

An opium den

Heroin and **cocaine** are two of the most dangerous drugs. They are illegal to sell or to use. Heroin comes from the opium poppy and cocaine comes from the **coca plant** (not to be confused with the **cacao plant** from which chocolate is made). The coca plant is native to Colombia in South America. Like morphine, cocaine is used as a painkiller. It was first used in 1883 as an **anaesthetic** but, like morphine, it is addictive.

A Garda seizure of cannabis

A person may become addicted to one of these drugs very quickly — perhaps with the first use or 'fix'. Heroin and cocaine both react with the chemicals that are naturally present in the brain. A person under the influence of such a drug may not know who they are or what they are doing. Addicts call this a **trip**. Once a trip is over, an addict may experience side-effects including sickness, confusion and pain. They may also experience a desperate need for more of the drug. They are addicted.

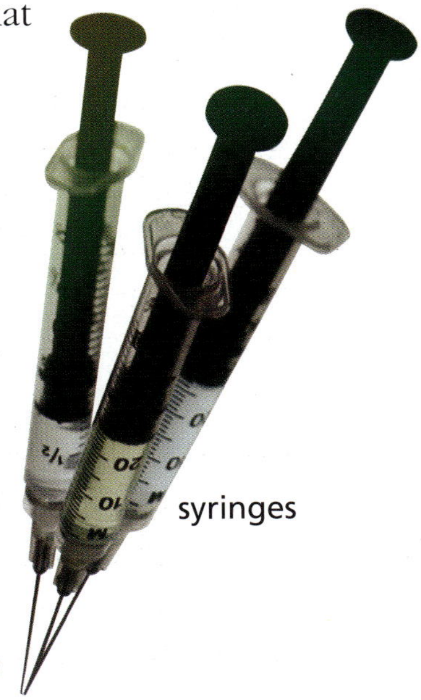

syringes

A Garda seizure of heroin

MATTER of FACT

The **Hashishin** were a group who terrorised parts of Persia and Syria in the 11th century. They got their name from the habit of taking the drug **hashish** before they attacked anyone. Hashish is also called **cannabis**. It is a plant that is smoked like tobacco but with different effects. From the word *Hashishin* we get the modern word *assassin*.

Drug trafficking

The term **drug trafficking** can mean growing the drug, transporting it, selling it to a drug user or encouraging people to abuse it. Drug trafficking is illegal.

Drugs such as opium, heroine and cocaine begin as crops grown by people who are desperate for money, usually in Third World countries. **Drug dealers** buy the crops for very little money and then process the plants into illegal drugs in hidden laboratories. Different people are hired to smuggle the drugs into countries. The smuggled drugs are sold to local drug dealers who use their network of **drug pushers** to sell the drugs for them. Sometimes, drug pushers will get drug addicts, in dire need of a fix, to sell the drugs themselves. Drug dealers always get other people to take the risks — they take all the profits.

Drugs are often smuggled on ships

MATTER OF FACT

In Ireland, the Gardaí co-operate with police in other parts of the world in tracking down drug traffickers. Specially trained **sniffer dogs** are available at airports and seaports to locate smuggled drugs. The Gardaí and the Naval Service have had great success in detecting drug traffickers. In spite of this, too many illegal drugs slip through the net.

Drugs smuggled inside a computer

Drug dealers are never concerned about health precautions. The drugs they sell are sometimes **contaminated**. Addicts using such drugs risk serious illness or even death. Certain drugs, such as heroin, are injected straight into veins using syringes. They usually damage the veins after a couple of injections. The addict must then try to locate more veins on his or her body, while ugly scars build up. Addicts often share syringes — this means the blood of one addict will mix with the blood of another. In this way, dangerous diseases are spread.

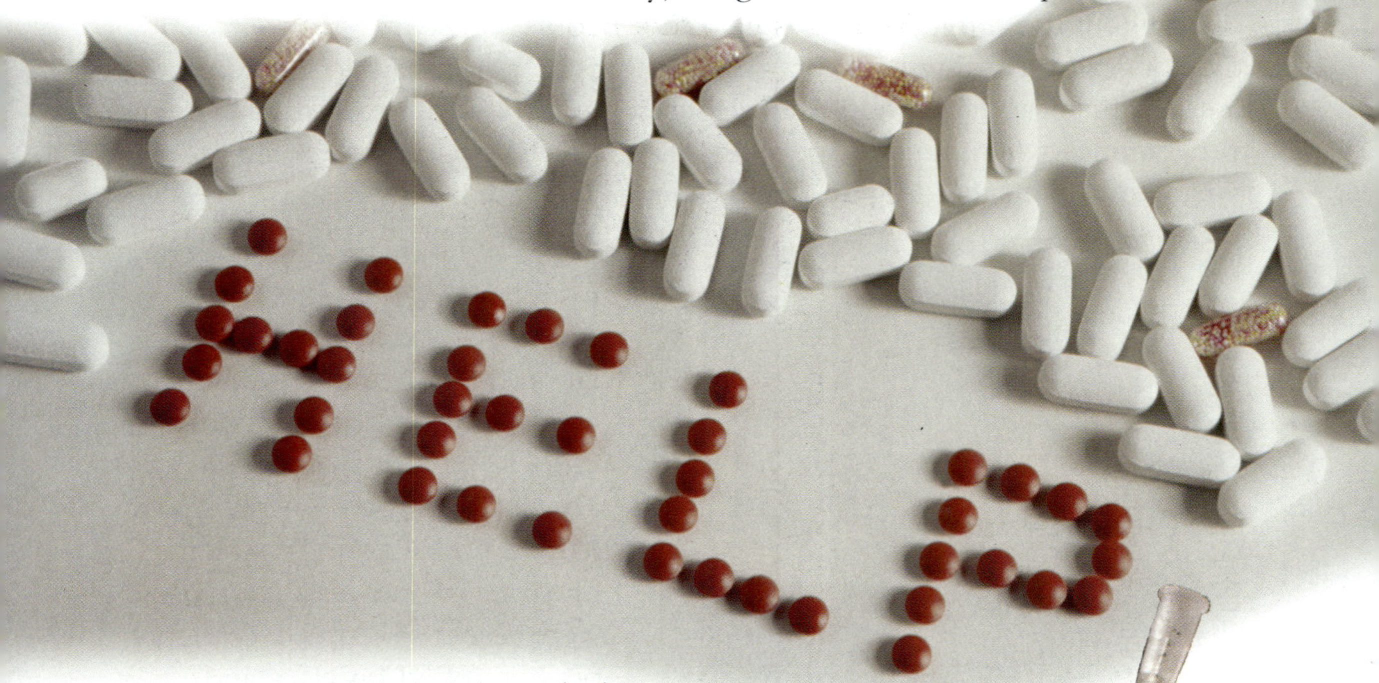

Some drugs are inhaled through the nose. A result of this is that the inside of the nose decays. Addicts are so desperate for a fix, however, that they will continue with this habit, no matter how much damage is caused.

As the addiction continues, the addict may need more and more of the drug to get the same effect. By this stage, there is a greater danger of the addict **overdosing** with the drug and dying.

heroin and a syringe

Many addicts attempt to give up their addiction. One method of doing this is called '**cold turkey**'. The addict suddenly stops taking the drug. What follows during cold turkey is indescribable agony and illness while the addict's body tries to readjust to life without the drug. Doctors call this misery **withdrawal symptoms**. For many addicts, cold turkey is too difficult to face. Help is available in the form of **detoxification programmes** where trained specialists give addicts legal drugs. This is to **wean** addicts off the drug and help them to **kick the habit**.

Drugs can be very expensive

Drugs are a major cause of crime in Ireland. A 1997 Garda report stated that sixty-six per cent of all detected thefts in the Dublin area were committed by drug users to pay for their addiction. This involved over twenty-seven million euros worth of stolen property in one year. Drug users were responsible for over eighty per cent of all **burglary** and muggings. The same report stated that 91 per cent of known drug addicts used heroin.

MATTER OF FACT

Drugs are very expensive. A drug pusher will often give the first fixes free or at a low price. However, once the victim is addicted, the cost of a fix goes up sharply. Many drug addicts resort to stealing to pay for their habit.

MATTER OF FACT

A journalist called Lanre Fehintola took heroin while writing about heroin addiction and its victims. He wanted to experience what life was like for an addict. He found out all too well — he was addicted to heroin for ten years.

MATTER OF FACT

If a drug addict gives birth to a child, that baby is born a drug addict. The baby must experience the misery of withdrawal symptoms during the first weeks of his / her life.

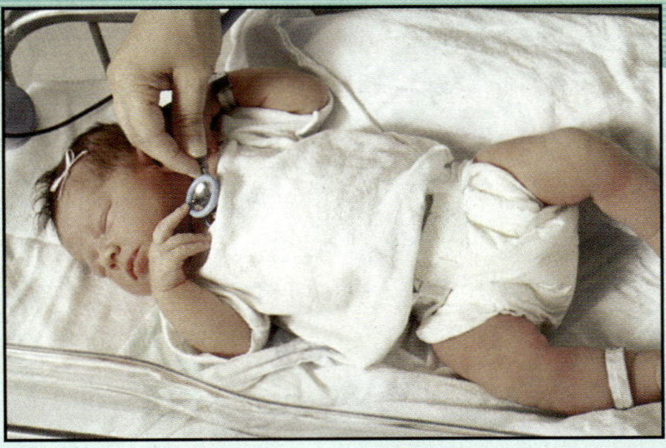

MATTER OF FACT

Cigarettes contain the drug **nicotine**. Nicotine is a legal drug, but is very addictive. Many people who smoke cigarettes find they cannot give them up. Cigarettes are known to be a major cause of lung cancer. Millions of deaths worldwide have been associated with cigarette smoking.

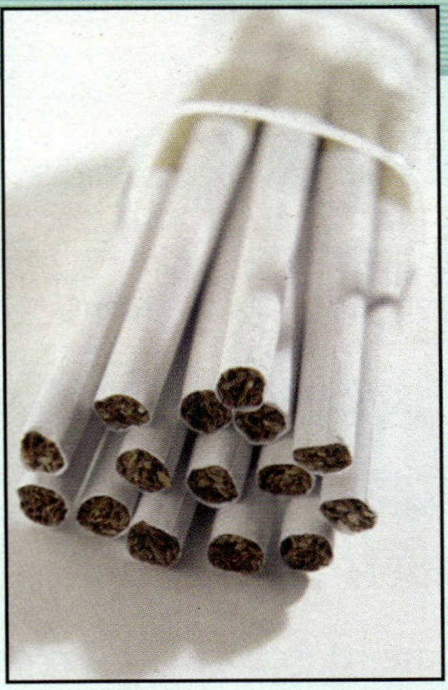

MATTER OF FACT

Alcohol is another legal drug that can be addictive. Alcohol addiction is known as alcoholism. As with other drug addicts, alcoholics require help to give up their habit.

More Blarney

1 Agree or disagree. Support your view with information you have.
- Cigarettes and alcohol are legal because they are not addictive.
- Without the problem of drug addiction, Ireland's crime rate would fall dramatically.
- It is easy to 'kick a drug habit'.
- Only illegal drugs cause misery and destruction.

2 Prepare and debate the motion 'Drugs do more harm than good'.

Tale and Detail

Complete the sentences. Write the answers in your copybook.

	A	B	C	D
Pharmaceutical companies make	farm machinery	drugs	cigarettes	plants
A chemical found in the periwinkle plant cures	cancer	measles	influenza	whooping cough
Cocaine comes from	the cacao plant	the coca plant	the poppy	chocolate
The Hashashin group got their name from	heroin	cocaine	ergot	hashish
Sniffer dogs are trained to	perform tricks	chase criminals	locate smuggled drugs	help the blind

Work to Discover

Name it! Read the clues completely before attempting to identify the drug.

1 It is one of the most dangerous drugs. 91% of known drug addicts use it.
2 It is found in cigarettes.
3 It sometimes grows in cereals. Eating it can cause personality change.
4 It was first used in 1883 as an anaesthetic. It is addictive.
5 It is made from the sap of the willow tree and was used by Ancient Greeks as a painkiller.
6 Doctors used it during the American Civil War to treat injured soldiers. It is used as a powerful painkiller today.
7 Another name for it is cannabis.

Word Wizardry

ph Read the hint and write the word containing the **ph** sound.

You bring a prescription here.	**When it rings, you answer it.**
Another name for a ghost.	**A ruler in Ancient Egypt.**
A mythical bird.	**A group of words but not a sentence.**
The first word in P.E.	**A camera can take one.**

What do you notice about the last word on the list? Do you know of any names with this sound? Make a class wall-chart of words containing **ph**.
Add more as you find them in your reading.

People A person who has a drug addiction is called an **addict**. Match the following words with the descriptions.

Bully	A person who hoards money
Widower	A person who saves another's life
Miser	A person who teases and taunts others
Hermit	A person who dies for a belief or cause
Victim	A person who is killed or injured by another
Martyr	A person who lacks courage
Hero	A person who lives in isolation
Coward	A man whose wife is dead

Find other similar words. Ask your partner to try to identify the word by listening to a clue.

Surf the Imagination

1. Write the case for and against the motion 'Cigarettes and alcohol should be made illegal'.
2. Imagine you are a scientist working on a cure for cancer. Write your diary entry for the night that you make a remarkable breakthrough in your research.
3. Imagine you are approached by a drug pusher, on the way home from school. How would you react? With your partner, improvise the conversation.
4. Design a poster to encourage people to give up smoking cigarettes or to avoid illegal drugs.

Mouse Search

1. Tea, coffee and Coca-Cola contain caffeine. Find out more about this drug.
2. Find out about the work of AA (Alcoholics Anonymous) and NA (Narcotics Anonymous).

Keeping afloat

In *The Spanish Donkey*, by Maeve Friel, Neil Hunt and 'Nacho' fly to Spain for the summer holidays. One of the oldest means of transportation is the boat. Read on to find out more about ships and shipping.

The other members of the hunting party looked on horrified as Brock slid down the riverbank and into the water below. All thoughts of killing the **mammoth** were forgotten. Some men dropped their flint headed spears and tried to reach him but it was too late. Brock was in the water now and none of the other hunters in the tribe could swim.

Brock himself screamed in terror, but his cries were cut short as he spluttered for breath in the water. He was surely doomed! Suddenly, his **flailing** arm struck a log that was being swept along beside him in the water. Brock grabbed onto the log and held it for dear life, weeping with relief. From the riverbank he could hear his friends cheering. He would live to hunt another day... and he had just discovered the boat!

Most historians agree that the first 'boats' were logs which people used to help them float across stretches of water. Not long after that, these logs were tied together to make rafts. These were the first steps in the **evolution** of ships and shipping.

A key development in the history of shipping was the ability to harness the wind. For 6 000 years, right up until the present day, sailing ships have used the wind to power them along. Here are some of the stages in the evolution of sailing ships.

Wind in your Sails

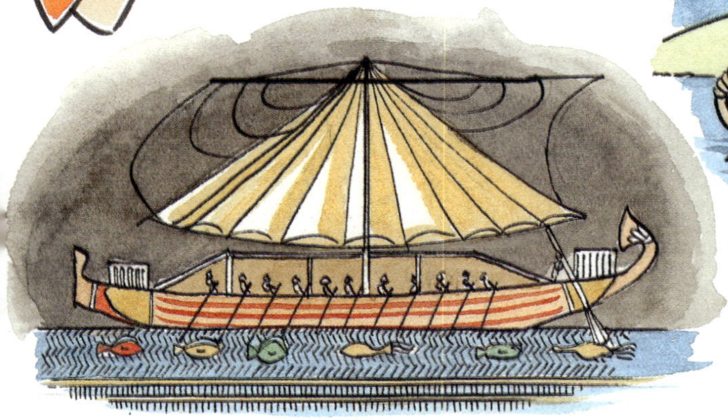

The Ancient Egyptians were using wind-powered ships on the river Nile as early as 2 500 BC.

The Greeks were sailing **triremes** like this as early as 500 BC. Triremes were powerful warships about thirty-six metres long. They used to sink enemy vessels by **ramming** them. Triremes were not powered by the wind alone. Several hundred slaves, chained up below deck, rowed the ships along using large oars.

The ancient Romans had a largy **navy** to help them rule their mighty empire. From around the 1st century AD, **galleys**, like this one were used in this navy. Like triremes, galleys were powered by the wind and by slaves.

Ships like this **dhow** were used in the Arab world more than 1 200 years ago. The dhow was so well-designed that ships based on the dhow model are still being built. Fictional characters like *Sinbad the Sailor* sailed in ships like dhows.

Around 1 000 AD, the Viking **longship** was the fastest vessel of its time. The Vikings used longships to carry out raids as far away as Russia, the Mediterranean and even North America.

Chinese **junks**, like this one, are still used by seafarers today. The Chinese built their ships with watertight compartments to prevent flooding and sinking. Some 800 years later, the *Titanic* was one of the first 'modern' ships to boast watertight compartments. Unfortunately, the *Titanic* sank on her maiden voyage.

When Christopher Columbus crossed the Atlantic in 1492, he did so with a **fleet** of three ships - the *Niña* and the *Pinta* and The *Santa Maria*. The three ships were not much bigger than fishing trawlers but they changed the world forever.

In the 18th and 19th centuries the British Royal Navy was the most powerful navy in the world. It was on the ***HMS Victory***, that Admiral Nelson beat Napoleon Bonaparte's French navy at the famous Battle of Trafalgar in 1805. *HMS Victory* is now preserved as a tourist attraction in Portsmouth, southern England.

During the 19th century, shipbuilders learned to build very fast vessels. These **clippers**, as they were called, were used to trade goods across the world. Many of them, such as the *Cutty Sark*, became record holders for speed.

Ships have played an important part in history. Developments at sea had a huge impact on events at home. The British created a huge empire using their navy to 'rule the waves'. Without those ships, they would never have conquered so many lands and changed the lives of so many people. Ships brought the Spanish to America. This invasion brought an end to the **Aztec** and **Inca** civilisations. It was ships that carried Africans as slaves to America and it was ships that brought British and Irish **convicts** to settle in Australia. As famine struck in Europe in the 1840s and 1850s, millions of people would escape by ship to North America, South America and New Zealand.

Ayers Rock, Australia

Shipbuilding also affected the land itself. Europe was once covered by lush forests. As many as one thousand trees were cut down to build one warship. As the kings and queens of Europe built up their naval forces to fight wars, the forests of Europe were slowly destroyed.

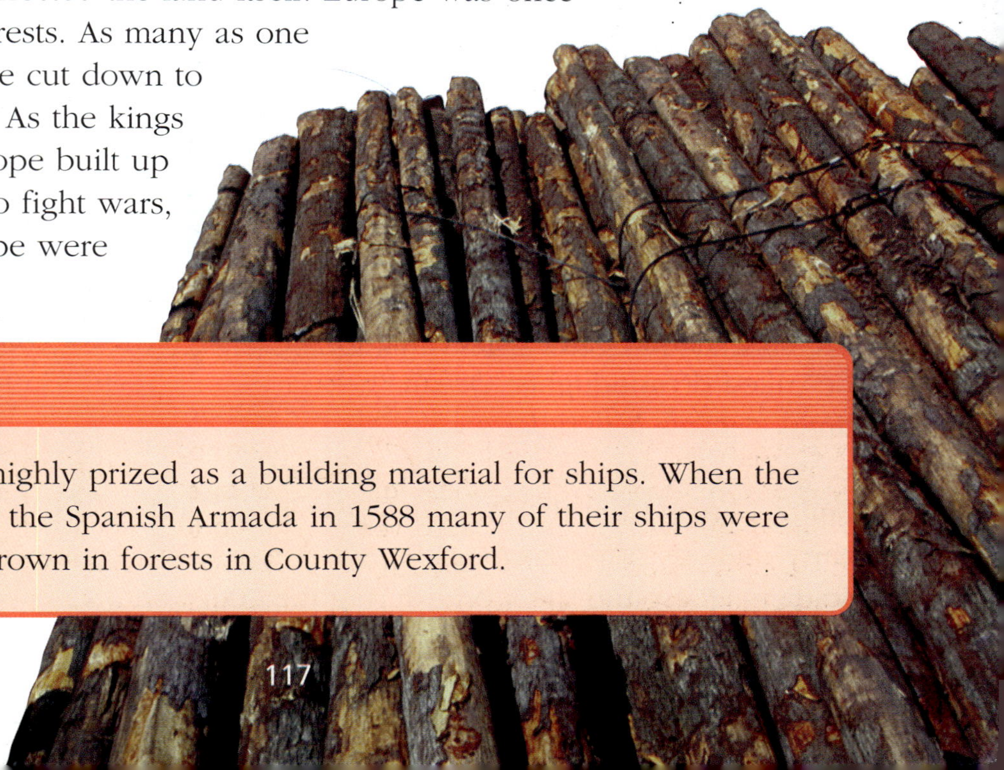

MATTER of FACT

Oak wood was highly prized as a building material for ships. When the English defeated the Spanish Armada in 1588 many of their ships were built from oak grown in forests in County Wexford.

On your own steam

The beginning of the 1800s saw the first ships that were powered by **steam**. The first steam-ship was built in 1807 by an American engineer Robert Fulton. It was called the *Clermont*. Early steam ships were really sailing ships with steam engines built into them. These ships 'crawled' through the water using large paddle wheels instead of **propellers**. Soon almost all ships were powered using steam and later by **diesel** power.

The first steam-ship to cross the Atlantic was the *Savannah*. She made the journey in 1819. The ship was actually powered by wind rather than steam for most of the voyage. The journey took the *Savannah* a month to complete, during which time the *steam engine* was used for only about eighty-five hours.

The construction of the iron ship, *Great Eastern*, 1838

The English engineer, Isambard Kingdom Brunel in 1845 designed the first ship that was built of iron. It was called *The Great Britain*. This new material was stronger and more **durable** than wood. This new development in shipping led to the launch of two new designs — the steel **battleship** *Dreadnought* and the fast **ocean liner** *Mauritania*. *Dreadnought* was such a success at the time that all battleships came to be called dreadnoughts. Ocean liners became a popular way to cross the Atlantic. The *Olympic*, the *Lusitania* and the *Titanic* are the most famous liners from that period. These ships, and others like them, would carry millions of poor **emigrants**, wealthy tourists, business people and soldiers all around the world during the 20th Century.

Unfortunately, the history of shipping has had its share of tragedy. Many shipping disasters have been the result of war. Some have been caused by carelessness. Others have been caused by flaws in the ships' design. **Marine engineers** all over the world are constantly working to make ships safer and more dependable.

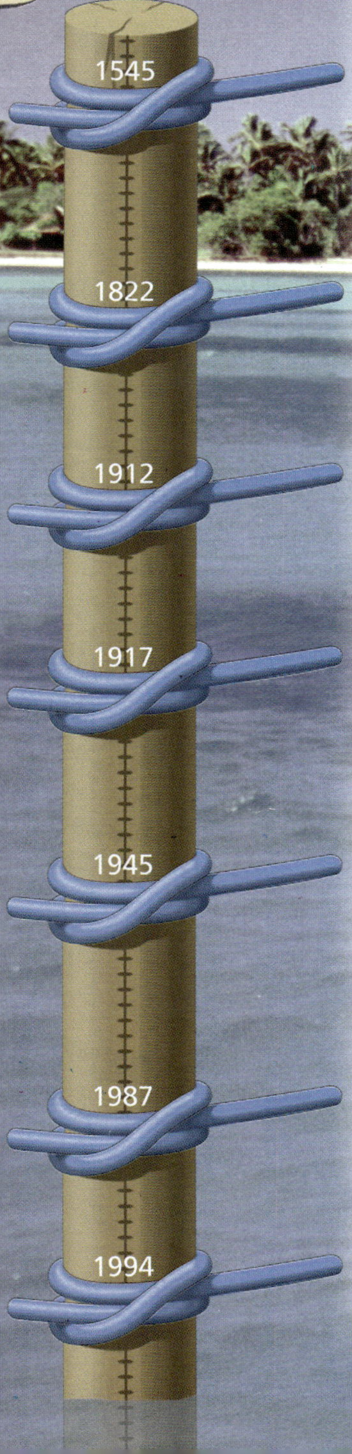

In 1545, the *Mary Rose*, the pride of King Henry VIII's navy, sank as she was leaving Portsmouth Harbour to do battle with the French. The ship had been overloaded with soldiers, cannons and **ammunition**. She had become top heavy and unstable. No one among the hundreds on board survived.

In 1822, a Chinese junk called the *Tek Sing* hit a **reef** and sank during a storm. There were up to 1 700 people on board. Only about 190 survived.

In 1912, the luxury liner, *Titanic*, collided with an iceberg and sank within two hours. 1 517 people died. 126 of them were Irish people who were emigrating to America to begin a new life.

In 1917, the passenger liner, the *Lusitania*, was **torpedoed** by a German submarine off the coast of Cork. 1 195 people died.

Up to 7 800 **refugees** died off the coast of Poland in January 1945 when the German liner *Wilhelm Gustloff* was torpedoed by a Soviet submarine. Ten days later, the same submarine would sink another German ship, the *Steuben*, with a loss of 3 000 lives.

Between 3 000 and 4 000 passengers on the Philippine ferry, the *Dona Paz*, died in December 1987 when the ship sank after being struck by an oil tanker.

The car ferry *Estonia* sank in heavy seas in the Baltic in 1994 with the loss of 909 lives.

Irish Ferries

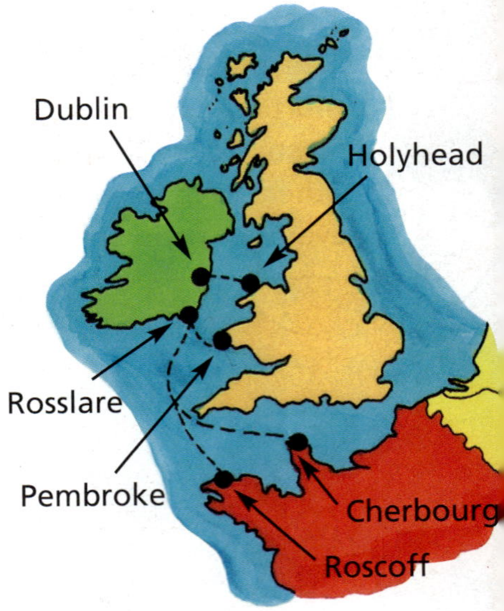

Ireland has its own ferry company, *Irish Ferries*. Their ships connect Ireland with Britain and France. Ships sail from Dublin and Rosslare in Ireland to Holyhead and Pembroke in Britain and to Cherbourg and Roscoff in France. The ships are designed to carry buses, cars and lorries as well as 'foot' passengers.

MV Isle of Inishfree

The *MV Jonathan Swift* (MV stands for 'marine vessel') was named after a famous Irish writer. It is the fastest vessel in the *Irish Ferries* fleet. It can travel over twice the speed of an ordinary car ferry

When it went into service, the *MV Isle of Inishfree* was the biggest car ferry to operate in northwest Europe. *Irish Ferries* decided to go one better than that and ordered the building of the world's biggest ferry ship, the *MV Ulysses*. This ship really is a monster! It is 208 metres long and can carry 1 300 cars

Matter of Fact

One of the oldest types of boats is the Irish **currach**. It is a long narrow boat used mainly in the west of Ireland.

Matter of Fact

In 1838, the steam ship *Sirius* was the first vessel to cross the Atlantic 'under its own steam', as the saying goes. It ran out of fuel before the crossing was completed. The crew had to burn furniture in the boilers to keep steam pressure up for the rest of the way!

Matter of Fact

Ship designers measure the size of a ship using a system called **displacement**. Displacement is the weight of water that a ship's **hull** pushes out of the way when it floats. A fishing boat might push away a few hundred tonnes. A car ferry might push away about 20 000 tonnes. A huge oil tanker, though, might push away 200 000 tonnes or more.

Matter of Fact

The Irish navy might not be the biggest in the world but each of its ships spends about six months of the year at sea. The US Navy and the British Royal Navy only spend half of that time at sea. Ireland is responsible for patrolling and protecting nearly 20% of the sea territory of the European Union. That means making sure that fishermen and sailors are safe and that criminals, such as drug smugglers, are caught.

More Blarney

1 Agree or disagree. Support your view with information you have.
   - Ships are a totally safe and dependable means of transport.
   - The development of shipping has had a major influence on world history.
   - Shipping saved much of Ireland's population in famine times.

2 With your partner, select what you think are the three most important developments in the history of shipbuilding.

Tale and Detail

1 What source of energy have sailing ships used for 6 000 years?
2 What happened at the Battle of Trafalgar?
3 How many trees were needed to build one warship?
4 Name three destinations of Irish Ferries.
5 How do designers measure the size of a ship?

Work to Discover

1 What do triremes and galleys have in common?
2 How do we know that dhows were well-designed?
3 Devise a game of 'Name The Ship' by re-reading the chapter and making-up clues for the names of ten ships. Then take turns with your partner, guessing the answers to each other's clues.

Example:

Clue: This ship was the pride of King Henry VIII's navy. She sank as she was leaving Portsmouth Harbour in 1545.
Answer: The Mary Rose.

Word Wizardry

Sometimes we devise rhymes to help us remember information e.g. ***'Thirty days has September...'***
We also use rhymes to help us remember dates e.g. ***'In fourteen hundred and ninety two, Columbus sailed the ocean blue.'*** Devise rhymes to help you remember the dates for the following events:

The sinking of the Titanic
The defeat of the Spanish Armada
The sinking of the Mary Rose
The crossing of the Atlantic by the Savannah
The Battle of Trafalgar
The building of the Clermont
The sinking of the Lusitania

Use this idea to help you to remember other important information.

Surf the Imagination

Either / Or

1 Write an eye-witness account of any of the tragedies listed on page 119 **OR** imagine you are a slave aboard a trireme or galley. Describe the conditions in which you work.

2 Design a poster for a travel agency, advertising an exotic world cruise aboard a luxury liner **OR** design a head for a Viking Longship.

3 Sing the round Row, Row, Row Your Boat **OR** make up the words and tune for a sea shanty.

Mouse Search

1 Many books have been based on the adventures of people who have been 'shipwrecked'. Find out who wrote the following books:

Robinson Crusoe
Gulliver's Travels
The Swiss Family Robinson
Island of the Blue Dolphins

2 Read **Sinbad, the Sailor** and other stories of the **Arabian Nights**.

3 Find out about the Inca and the Aztec civilisations.

Final Answer

The world's biggest ferry ship is called?

A The MV Jonathan Swift
B The Sirius
C The Mauritania
D The MV Ulysses

A

addiction a habit that is very difficult to give up, for example taking drugs or gambling

advance party a group of people sent to a location before the main group arrives

agriculturalist a person who is skilled in cultivating land

air raid a bomb attack on a town or city by aircraft

anaesthetic a drug that prevents patients from feeling pain during operations

antihistamine a drug used in dealing with allergic reactions

antiseptic a substance that kills germs

archer a person who uses a bow and arrow

asthma a medical condition which makes a person experience difficulty when breathing

autobiography the story of a person's life that is written by that person

Aztecs people who ruled Mexico before the Spanish invaded the country in the 16th century

B

Band Aid a famine relief programme organised by Bob Geldof in 1984 to raise money for famine victims in Ethiopia

battleship a large, heavily-armed warship

bog holes a hole containing soft mud or quicksand, sometimes filled with water

Braille a system of writing or printing using raised dots that blind people 'read' with their fingers

brain damage a temporary or permanent injury to, or disease of, the brain

C

camouflage a disguise that makes something look like part of its surroundings

cannabis a plant used as a drug for its intoxicating effect. Also known as 'hashish'

canter a gentle gallop

Caravaggio an Italian artist who lived in the 16th and early 17th centuries and painted *The Taking of Christ*

cold turkey the symptoms following the sudden withdrawal of a drug from a person who has been addicted to the drug

cold war a situation where countries are political enemies but are not openly fighting each other

D

detoxification programme a programme designed to help drug addicts to remove all drugs from their systems and give up the habit of taking drugs

drought a long period without any rain

drug dealers people who process crops into illegal drugs and then smuggle the drugs into other countries

drug pushers people who encourage other people to buy or sell drugs

duet a piece of music written for two performers

E

eaves the overhanging edges of a roof

emigrants people who move to another country to live

enlisted joined the army

excavated uncovered something by digging, especially in building or archaeology

F

famine a severe shortage of food, resulting in widespread disease and starvation

Fertile Crescent an area now known as the Middle East, that could once support large amounts of crops

footings small pyramids formed by sods of drying turf

fossil fuel fuels such as coal, oil and peat that are formed over thousands of years from the remains of plants and animals

G

Geronimo famous Apache warrior who fought invading soldiers in the 1860s

H

host a living creature on which another living creature is growing and reproducing

Hussey, Philip an 18th century Irish portrait painter

I

Ice Age a long period of time when a great part of the Earth's surface was covered by ice

Incas South American Indians who ruled part of the Andes Mountains in the 15th and early 16th centuries until the Spanish invasion in 1532

Irish Free State twenty-six counties of Southern Ireland that were part of the British Commonwealth from 1921 until 1937

Irish National Stud a place where Irish horses are bred, and which is one of Ireland's principal tourist attractions

J

Jellett, Mainie A 20th century Irish artist who worked in the Cubist style

jodhpurs trousers that fit closely from the knee to the ankle, worn by horse riders

K

knighted to be granted a title of nobility

L

landscape a painting that depicts an area of land, rather than people, buildings or objects

larvae an insect in the first stage of its life after it comes out of the egg

League of Nations an organisation founded by forty countries in 1919 and whose role was to prevent wars from breaking out

limestone a soft rock formed over millions of years by fused layers of shells and skeletons

Live Aid concerts in London and Philadelphia organised by Bob Geldof in 1985 to raise money for famine victims in Ethiopia

longbow a large bow and arrow; the main weapon of the English army from the 14th century until the introduction of firearms

louse a small insect that infests the hair and skin of humans and animals

Louvre Museum an art museum in Paris, France

M

Maclise, Daniel a 19th century Irish painter whose painting *The Marriage of Strongbow and Aoife* depicts the Norman invasion of Ireland in the 12th century

malaria fever a disease, spread by mosquitoes, that kills more people every year than any other infectious disease

marine engineers people who design ships and submarines

moccasins shoes made of deerskin or other soft leather, traditionally worn by North American Indians

Mona Lisa a portrait painted by the Italian artist, Leonardo da Vinci

Monet, Claude a French 19th century artist and one of the early Impressionist painters

morphine a powerful painkiller made from refined opium

N

Native Americans the earliest inhabitants of North America, often referred to as American Indians

nicotine an addictive substance found in tobacco

no man's land an area between two enemy trenches on a battlefield that is occupied by neither side

Norman Knights warriors from Scandinavia who settled in Normandy in Northern France and who later conquered England and Ireland

O

O'Conor, Roderic a 19th century Irish artist whose paintings were greatly influenced by Impressionism

opiates strong drugs made from refined opium

overdose a dangerously large amount of a drug or medicine

P Q R

paddock a small field used for keeping horses

peace treaty an agreement between once warring countries or factions

plankton tiny creatures that float in the sea and lakes

portrait a painting, photograph or sculpture that depicts one person or a small group of people

quiver a long container used to hold arrows

S

siege the action of surrounding a place with an army until the inhabitants surrender

sniffer dogs dogs trained to smell and discover drugs and explosives

T

tacked up putting on a horse's riding harness, saddle, bridle etc.

táin an Irish word meaning 'cattle'

thoroughbred a pure-bred animal whose ancestry can be traced back generations

torpedo an underwater missile that explodes on impact with its target

trenches a long narrow cut in the earth, often used in warfare as a cover for troops

trip though usually meaning a journey, this word can also mean the hallucinations experienced when taking a drug

truce an agreement between warring parties to stop fighting

U

United Nations an organisation founded after World War II that acts as a 'referee' between warring countries

USSR the name for Russia from 1922 until 1991

V W X Y Z

veteran an experienced solider, usually of a particular war

wean to gradually let go of a habit

withdrawal symptoms discomfort experienced by a person who gives up something, for example drugs

Yeats, John Butler a 19th century Irish portrait painter